HORSE and CART DAYS

Memories of a farm boy

by A B Tinsley

First published 1976 by Onny Press (ISBN 0 905019 02 4)
as WITH HORSE AND CART AND FRIEND

REPUBLISHED NOVEMBER 1990 by CLARK AND HOWARD BOOKS
4 Merridale Gardens,
Wolverhampton, WV3 OUX

Typed by Hilary Clark

Printed by Rank Xerox Copy Centre

Drawings from memory, by the Author

ISBN 0 9509555 8 2

To JOAN

whose help and encouragement
coupled with her abiding affection
for Shropshire
made these reminiscences possible

CONTENTS

		Page
1	FARM HOUSE DAYS	5
2	FARMYARD IMPRESSIONS	14
3	BROADER PICTURES	24
4	WORK AND PLAY	31
5	COMMON FLOK	37
6	SEASONAL ARTS AND SKILLS	42
7	HAY HARVEST	48
8	CORN HARVEST	52
9	ROOT HARVEST AND WINTER TASKS	58
A SECRET JOY		65
LIST OF ILLUSTRATIONS		66
GLOSSARY		67

STONE HOUSE FARM - HOPTON

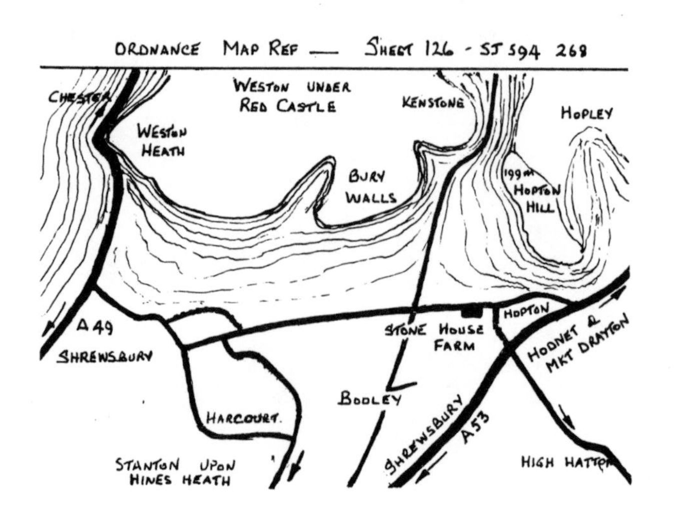

1

FARM HOUSE DAYS

I remember, I remember,
The house where I was born ...

T. Hood

A farmhouse must surely be one of the more pleasant places to claim as one's birthplace. For me, the farm at Hopton, north-east of Shrewsbury, conjours up a host of happy memories, accumulated during the impressionable years of my childhood and early manhood, during and after the 1914-1918 war. Whenever I choose to indulge in a flight of thought back to that period, I see in my mind's eye that substantial, and not unattractive, house, built of cut stone, and partially covered with ivy and appropriately named STONE HOUSE. It seemed to stand so squarely against all the winds that blew.

Architecturally it conformed to the general pattern of most farm houses, with its large rooms, solid beams, quarried floors and extensive dairy cellar.

There was no furniture in the kitchen which did not serve a useful purpose in the everyday life of the farm. Some of it was by no means small, yet there seemed to be a vast amount of space left in which to move around, even allowing for a built-in copper alongside the highly polished cooking range. The shining blackness of this range contrasted cozily with the dull red well-scrubbed tile of the floor.

What eons of time and plenitude of work went into the weekly black-leading of that range and the daily scrubbing of the floor. The kitchen was the most used room of the house, and it was always comfortable according to the seasons.

In winter the brightly leaping orange and yellow flames licked around the bottom of the great iron kettle, hanging from a hook, or 'swake.' The contents of the kettle bubbled cheerily with a low murmur, acting as background music to the good burr of our Shropshire tongue.

In summer these sounds were augmented by another, the lazy

buzzing of flies at the window, through which the sunlight streamed in a great pool, turning a square patch of red tiling to a subtle rose tint.

The ceiling was low, and hooks in the white beams held various guns, used mostly for keeping down vermin such as rabbits and wood pigeon, although these, of course, also augment farm diet.

There was a three-cornered, chunky oak cupboard standing in one corner of this room, its top doors too high for a small boy to reach, and behind these were countless odd items, such as bottle medicines and cattle remedies, too dangerous for a child's meddlesome fingers.

Another useful item consisted of a robust rack which was slung just below the ceiling and usually carried one or two sides of bacon. Two or three hurricane lamps also hung from beams near the back door, and these were always kept clean and full of paraffin.

As a rule there were also two or three large hams in clean linen bags hung from beams near the walls. This home-cured ham was always a feature of Sunday morning breakfast - together with strong coffee brewed from berries ground in a coffee mill, which was attached to the end of the big beam running across the top of an ingle recess.

A final touch of utilitarianism was the stone sink, cool, shallow, and always damp, fitted into one corner of the kitchen, to which we boys were firmly directed before each meal, or upon entering the kitchen from the fields.

Only with well-scrubbed hands were we then allowed to seat ourselves at the great, equally well-scrubbed table, which in the harvest season could seat ten men. This table was placed just in front of the window and opposite to my grandmother's old rocker, which was always set close to the hob. This was her favourite spot, for not only was it warmest in winter, but to the end of her days she had a partiality for scalding cups of weak tea without sugar or milk. From her chair she could brew it with a minimum of effort from the ever-bubbling kettle.

My early memories are of the extraordinary degree of self-support which existed in those days. Food was largely a product of the farm. Bread was baked twice a week and other groceries laid in in good quantity, especially before the winter set in. Fruit and vegetables were preserved and kept in a special store room. Medicaments were kept for almost every contingency, both for humans and animals, some being known only by the name of the local person who made them. There was, for example, 'BESSIE PYE'S SALVE' and 'JANE LEECHES' OINTMENT.'

The dairy and rock-hewn beer cellar were both entered initially by the same door, situated near the back door and in a short passage leading into the kitchen itself. Upon opening this door one had the option of taking three steps ahead and down, to arrive on the spotless red-tiled floor of the dairy, or of turning right and taking seven or eight steps down to the cellar.

The far end of the dairy was occupied by a large 'salting' stone, cut from hard sandstone, and suitably excavated to a depth of some five inches, including a drainhole at one corner. The stone rested upon brick supports to bring its height some two-and-a-half feet above the floor level. Upon this, during winter months, it was a common sight to see flitches and hams being cured under a liberal coating of common salt.

The rest of the dairy was mainly devoted to milk and butter making, though some shelves were used as a larder.

My earliest memories are of large shallow pans set out on the floor and on special benches, waiting for the cream to rise on the milk which each contained.

The cellar was quite large and almost dark, but it was just possible to see the brick-built stillage across one end. This could hold four thirty-six-gallon barrels. Since it was cut in sandstone bed-rock, the cellar maintained a uniformly low temperature - ideal for keeping beer in perfect condition for any length of time.

In those days beer was provided at all major farming operations, such as hay harvest, corn harvest and on threshing days. Beer drinking was, therefore, a custom, and not a habit, so that it was quite usual for grown-ups to draw a glass of beer at any time if they so desired.

Visitors would seldom depart without being asked if they would like a glass of beer. This fact was well-known, and some, I am sure, called purposely; or, like the miller's waggoner, would make enough noise about the buildings to attract attention to their presence and thirst.

The front room or dining room was as large as the kitchen and was well-filled with good solid furniture, which included a friendly old grandfather clock, marking the passing of the minutes with a most solemn tick - a tick which seemed to strike sympathetic vibrations with the howling of the wind on stormy winter nights.

Certain rooms were forbidden territory to a small toddler, including the dairy and cellar, together with a snug little parlour located over the cellar, and the apple closet upstairs. Also upstairs were the bedrooms - quite large, with the exception of two, one of which was occupied by a workman who lived in. Though the larger bedrooms had reasonably large windows, there was provision for the insertion of extra ones should they ever be deemed necessary. This fact was evident from the location of properly masoned stone sills visible from the outside of the house. Windows had not been fitted at the time of building, in 1841, because of the window tax of those days.

Our water was drawn from a fearsomely deep draw-well situated on a 'causey' or paved yard, adjacent to the back door. The mechanism of the well was quite ingenious, being a five-gallon bucket at either end of the long draw-chain, which passed over a large chain-wheel, while the bucket at the top and in use stood on the pair of doors covering that side of the wellshaft. When the bucket needed refilling, it was lifted aside while the doors were opened upwards so that it could be lowered to the full extent of the slack chain.

When the doors closed the chain passed through a diamond-shaped orifice cut half into the abutting edges of each door section.

The bucket was raised by means of the usual handle, which turned the main chain-wheel through a simple reduction gear, while an essential device, in the form of a falling ratchet or 'dog', prevented the winding handle from spinning round in a reverse direction, if grip were lost on it.

A TWO-BUCKET WELL

Needless to say I was never permitted to go anywhere near this dangerous installation, and, upon consideration, it must have presented a very real safety hazard in my parents' opinion, since it was not possible to safeguard it in any practical way.

I can remember them saying, "If you go too near the well, Black Sam will have you."

My father even used to hold imaginary conversations with this forbidding, if mythical, character, when I ventured too near. He would lift the door and call into the cool, echoing depths, that a little boy was getting too venturesome. A fearsome prickle would tingle my spine as a gruff, sepulchral voice echoed in response. "Tell him to be off quickly as I am looking for a nice fat little boy."

This method of distraction worked most effectively because I remember having visions of some inky octopus-like creature, lurking in those murky dripping depths, waiting for just such a boy as me.

Curiously enough the well was frequently consulted as a barometer. Whenever the question of weather arose, as it so often does on a farm, someone was sure to ask, "What does the well say?" In fact it 'said' quite a lot if one interpreted its behaviour correctly, because it 'blew up' for stormy weather, and 'drew down' for fine weather. When the well was 'doing nothing,' the weather could generally be classed as fair or changeable.

The draught of air which produced this phenomenon passed through crevices in the doors and particularly strongly through the diamond-shaped chain-holes.

With the bucket standing at the top, over the one chain-hole it was quite easy to decide what the well was 'doing,' either by placing a hand over the open chain-hole or by putting a lighted match or straw over it. Before and during very stormy weather it was possible to hear the uprush of air making a noise as it passed through the water-filled crevices.

Where the air came from, or where the down-draught went to, no one ever discovered, but it was assumed that it was caused by some fault or discontinuity in the lower rock strata, which gave access to caves somewhere. Even so, rare expeditions to the bottom of the well to retrieve lost buckets never resulted in the finding of any hole or cleft.

On this same well-yard were several large stone 'cesterns' (cisterns) used to contain pig food, which largely consisted of the skim milk from the dairy. The actual pigsties were situated over a burrstone wall and included several well-made sties and 'inlets' all of which could be opened onto an open 'outlet' or free run.

The close proximity of pigs to the farmhouse would not conform to modern ideas of hygiene, but it was most convenient in many ways and in any case the pigs were happy enough.

One day I was standing on some planks used to cover the cisterns, when there was a splintering sound as they collapsed

- decanting me into the pig food. The clinging smell of sour milk and the fact that I was prematurely sent to bed while my clothes were washed, combined to make it a day NOT to be remembered.

A mixed bag of memories centre around the somewhat rustic type of lavatory, which was of the simplest earth-type and located, so it seemed, VERY far away from the house. Screened by a box hedge and shielded by damson trees, it could not justly lay clain to any architectural beauty. The interior displayed extreme austerity; in fact only one concession to convenience was made, and that was a 'two-holer' seat. This somewhat crude example of a carpenter's work had the holes cut in two sizes, apparently to indicate the deeper workings of some erstwhile rustic mind.

Visits to this secluded spot could be pleasant or otherwise, dependant on the season of the year. The song of the birds, the hum of bees, the aromatic sharp scent of the box hedge, and the whisperings of the surrounding foliage could easily lure one to prolong the stay in summer. On the other hand, in severe winter weather, when frost and snow and howling gales prevailed, no one occupied the place very long, and a nocturnal expedition, with the aid of a flickering hurricane lamp, was something to which more than passing thought was given.

Another building on the well-yard or 'causey' was known as the 'bakehouse,' which also housed a large, thirty-six-gallon copper used for brewing and for heating water on the occasions when a pig was killed - when quantities of scalding water were needed to facilitate the removal of bristles which had to be scraped off the dead animal.

The bake oven was an old wood-fired type, with a hemispherical interior. It could be used for either baking or roasting joints of meat, but required some experience to adjust for temperature.

On brewing days I spent many cozy hours in this little retreat, sitting quietly on a stool in the semi-darkness, watching red-hot cinders fall into the ashpit and listening to the low-piched simmer of a scalding brew, which my father kept gently on the move by means of an oar-shaped mash paddle. Sometimes we baked potatoes in the ash-hole and these always seemed more tasty than any baked indoors.

Brewing thirty-six gallons was, for us, a day-and-a-half job. Work started by cleaning and assembling the necessary utensils, while the copper, full of water, was heating.

The big mash tub was set up on a special bench just outside the door, and into this a specific quantity of malt was 'shot' or tumbled. The quantity of malt was varied according to the strength of the beer required. An extra strong drop was always brewed for Christmas.

Scalding water was added to the malt and left for a period while infusion was taking place. When this was complete, the straw-coloured, aromatic liquid was drawn off and returned to the copper, there to be brought to a simmering heat before the hops were added. At this stage a careful watch had to be kept to prevent the brew from boiling over.

During this period the residual malt, or 'grains,' were decanted from the mash tub into a pig-cistern and the tub cleaned in readiness to receive the brew for cooling.

Hop leaves were removed by pouring the brew through a hair-sieve lodged across the top of the mash tub - an operation which brought an end to the day's brewing.

The following morning, when the temperature of the liquid had fallen to barely tepid, the barm had to be added to start fermentation. Barm was circulated freely among neighbours since it did not keep very long, and anyone brewing automatically kept a fresh supply in case a neighbour required any.

The word 'barm' always reminds me of another substance not unlike the true one, but known as 'beggar's barm.' This could quite often be seen after a heavy storm, when flood water had rushed over dry, dusty soil, or down wheel-ruts, fast enough to create a froth.

True barm is the product of yeast or the result of adding yeast originally for fermentation purposes. It multiplies very quickly during fermentation and this froth is nearly all waste since a very small quantity will start a new fermentation.

If the temperature was correct, fermentation was rapid, any excess liquid frothing up over the rim of the tub and running away to waste. But in two or three hours fermentation would have ceased and the new beer could then be transferred to a freshly prepared barrel in the cellar where it could be kept palatable indefinitely.

The subject of brewing brings to mind an occasion when a neighbouring farmer obtained a replacement barrel for brewing, and his first brew turned out to be more than potent, and also exceptionally palatable. It wasn't until some time later that he admitted to using an old secondhand rum cask without first washing it out. In his droll way, he opined that it could be the spirit absorbed into the wood which had something to do with its popularity and the convivial atmosphere among those assisting on his threshing day.

The bake oven was primarily intended for the baking of bread, but, with the advent of a baker's delivery round, the duties of the oven diminished. Apart from being used for an occasional batch of bread, its other use was for baking pork pies - a job which followed the killing of a pig.

This oven was heated by means of a wood or stick fire actually kindled inside it using dry, non-resinous materials, such as hazel, birch, alder and oak.

WOOD-FIRED BAKE OVEN

Fire was maintained with sufficient fuel to raise the heat until the arching roof bricks appeared white and the embers reduced to a glowing mass covering the oven bottom. At this stage all the ash was carefully raked out by means of a special scraper and deposited in the ashpit below.

Meanwhile the loaves or pies had been prepared and were ready to be slid into the oven-chamber, each one being carefully placed on the oven bottom by means of a special oven slice, rather like a flat iron spade with a four-foot-long handle.

The access door was put back in position, the damper pushed in, and then the baking was done. It always seemed that a special flavour was imparted to whatever was baked in this way. Our own pies were made with spare pork and fat, but this was not minced. Instead it was cut into small cubes (not cooked) and put into the crust in the ratio of three parts pork to one part fat. This spare pork was any which needed removal in the dressing of hams and flitches to tidy them up before 'salting.'

Before the pie-top was crimped on, a few slices of cooking apple were laid over the filling so that the juice percolated throughout the pie - delicious eating!

Pigs which were reared and killed for household use were large and consequently fat. Accumulation of fat around the animal's kidneys was known as the 'leaf' and was converted into pure lard by the simple process of cutting it into small cubes and rendering it down in a massive cast-iron, three-legged pot, hung from the swinging angle-iron over the kitchen fire.

Many a meal was made from this same lard spread on toast and eaten hot or cold, while the residue from rendering down was known as 'scratchings' which, when eaten cold with pepper and vinegar, were equally delicious - the REAL scratchings.

RENDERING DOWN LARD

(The three-legged pot was probably made in Ironbridge)

2

FARMYARD IMPRESSIONS

God gave men all the earth to love,
But since our hearts are small,
Ordained for each, one spot should prove
Beloved over all.

Rudyard Kipling

Interest in these more domestic aspects of farm life began to fade as I started to absorb the wider environments of the farmyard and outlying fields, and in the company of some older person was allowed to make tours around the premises.

All the farm buildings were stone, and apart from the cow sheds all had hay lofts which were well stocked before the onset of winter.

The stable loft was entered by a vertical ladder beside one of the mangers and hay could be pushed down to each horse's rack as required.

Our granary was entered by means of a flight of stairs from the barn and opened out on either side. To the left of the stairhead was stored the ground corn returned from the local mill. To the right, the corn yet to be ground.

Most of the grain was stored in large wooden bins or 'witches' capable of holding about two tons each. This method of storage was used in an effort to minimise the use of sacks, in which rats and mice constantly nibbled holes to get at the contents.

Any sacks which were used and which had become holed had to be repaired, and this was a task reserved for wet days. When I grew older I spent many an hour diligently darning away with a special sack needle, while listening to the drum-beat of the rain as it tattooed on the roof.

As the farm kitchen was the hub of farm life indoors, so was the barn the centre of outdoor activity.

All the handtools, and also a fairly comprehensive selection of maintenance tools, including a small anvil and vice, were kept in there, plus portable platform scales for weighing corn

1 RICK KNIFE (Loose hay or straw rick cutting)
2 ALL WOOD HAY RAKE
3 THATCHER'S COMB
4 HEEL RAKE (Stubble cleaning)
5 GIN TRAP (Rabbits & vermin)
6 SHORT HANDLED HEDGE KNIFE (Hedge bank trimming)
7 LONG HANDLED HEDGE KNIFE
8 BARREL TYPE MOLE TRAP (Wood)

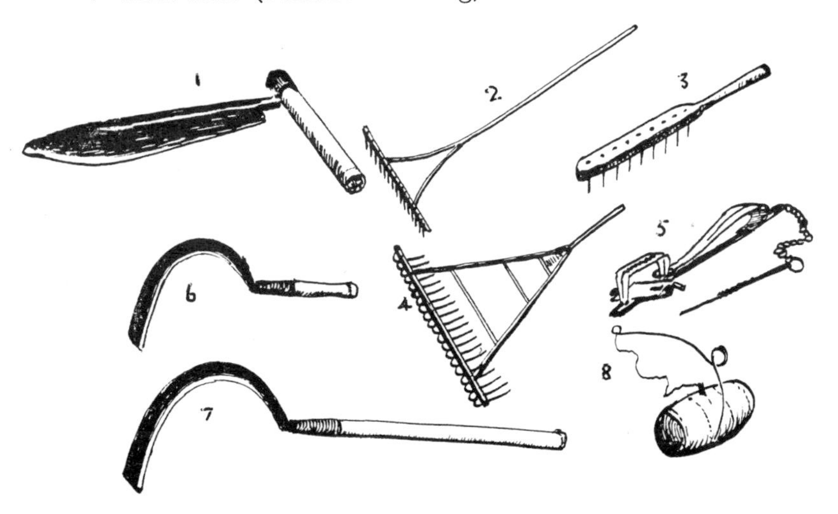

or potatoes.

Implements were kept under cover in an implement shed, as were carts and lorries, when not in use. Those needing repair were taken to the local blacksmith, who was a most versatile man capable of shoeing horses, hooping cartwheels and forge-welding broken parts.

I always liked to be taken along on a visit to the blacksmith, where I could watch him dexterously plying his craft, see the glowing fire and the sparks fly as he worked the white-hot metal, and listen to the tinkle and thud as he varied the weight of his hammer blows - how easily he made the metal assume some required shape or joined two pieces together whilst at a sizzling white heat.

Sometimes I would even be allowed to operate his bellows, by raising and lowering an arm attachment which was finished off at the handle end with a curved cow's horn, which provided a smooth and handy grip.

Around the walls hung sets of horseshoes, fashioned to fit individual farm horses belonging to the blacksmith's customers.

Shoeing was done in what was called the 'penthouse,' and memories of the acrid smell of burned hoof still linger -

together with the smith's kindly words as he soothed horses which resented being shod.

Our cow houses were at right angles to the main barn and stables. The enclosure formed by these and the pig sties was occupied by the 'mixen,' which at the start of the winter was empty, but rapidly filled up when all the stock were indoors. All mixens conformed to the same idea, being nothing more than a hollow or hole around which the stables and cattle sheds were arranged, allowing for sufficient walkway. Cleaning out dung and litter was, therefore, easier since it only needed to be tumbled downhill into the mixen.

At the rear of the cow houses, but accessible to them, was the turnip house where food for both milking cows and fattening bullocks was prepared. During the winter this place had to be continually replenished with either turnips or mangols, ready at hand for feeding into the pulpers and mixing with the other dry feed.

Cattle tied in stalls or kept in loose-boxes or stockyard could not fend for themselves, and feeding was therefore a compulsory task which required a supply of food to be readily available regardless of the weather.

Before being allowed to enter stables and cowsheds, I was always warned to keep well clear of the animals' hind feet, because, being small, I could easily be mistaken for a dog trotting along behind them. But, in spite of this warning, I was once laid low by a well-placed kick between the eyes from a mature milking cow, one summer evening. This unkind act resulted in my being rushed indoors to have attention in the shape of rural first-aid, which culminated in my going to bed with a vinegar and brown paper dressing on the bruise.

Cow-kine, as most farming folk know, are curious creatures. they can become as friendly and affectionate as a 'cade' lamb, if given encouragement, yet they never get on such terms with each other. Though they keep together in small or large herds, there is always an order of seniority which is rigidly adhered to, as can be seen when a herd passes through a gateway.

Perhaps this order of leadership springs from a female tendency to exaggerate the importance of minor matters. The old bull amongst the herd didn't give two hoots whether he came first or last through the gate.

During winter months, all the cattle were kept indoors at night and food was fed to them in their 'booseys' or cribs, in the form of pulped turnip, hay or crushed corn. The safe 'folding' of all the cattle on a stormy winter night always sent a thrill through me. It seemed like the pulling of a castle drawbridge, signifying that all within the walls were safe and cared for.

Just before bedtime, a visit would be paid to all the animals in their various buildings, to ensure that they were safe and in no danger from their tethers, that is, that they were not hanging in their tie-chains.

On frosty nights the warm, turnip-sweet breath of each animal would rise, like steam from a kettle. The chinking of tie-chains, puffs and snorts, all contributed to the picture illuminated by the ubiquitous hurricane lamp at this important time of 'supping up,' as it was known.

A day of paramount interest was when the threshing machine came. Its arrival resembled a small circus coming to town. The 'machine,' or thresher, usually arrived in the evening before the work was to begin, in time to 'set-up' alongside the rick, ready for an early start the following morning.

I marvelled at the way the driver manoeuvered such large pieces of equipment which, apart from the steam traction engine, included the threshing box; a baler; a binder; and a large caravan - in that order.

Setting up a threshing box and the engine to drive it was very tricky, especially on uneven ground. To work efficiently the box had to stand level and the steam engine had to take up a position in the rear, and in line - sufficiently near for the driving belt to reach from the fly-wheel to the driving pulley on the box. The engine was never left near the ricks overnight because of the risk of fire.

In the morning, when everything was ready and the thatch removed from the corn rick, the engine driver would give a blast on the whistle to call the workmen together, and the day's work would commence. Hour after hour the reliable old engine steadily puffed away at the pre-set governed speed, and sheaf after sheaf of corn would be fed into the drum of the threshing box.

At the far end of the box the straw was ejected, either to be tied into battens with binder twine, or to be baled after being crushed and compressed into a heavy wad, and then fastened with wire. At the end nearest the engine, corn would steadily fall into sacks from different spouts according to the quality selected and set by adjustments to the machine's sampling drum.

Many pleasant hours were spent standing beside the engine as 'she' steadily drove the complex chain of tackle at the correct and unvarying speed. The big flashing connecting rod and wobbling valve gear seemed tireless, while the spinning

STEAM THRESHING MACHINE

governor rapidly corrected any effect of varying load. The hiss of escaping steam and the crackle of drops of water as they dripped from steam glands onto the hot casing; the radiated warmth from the engine, especially on a cold day; the swirling smoke and dust; the steady hum from the box - all this was part of a big day in a little boy's life.

But, undoubtedly, the best part of the day came when, towards the end of the work, hosts of mice and even rats, began to escape into the open. Armed with a sturdy thatch peg, I joined in a scurry with others of the neighbouring children who happened to be around, in meting out death to these pests. This orgy of destruction was always accompanied by shrieks, yells and much laughter, and while it may seem that our amusement was cruel, it was very necessary to the running of the farm that at least the numbers of these small creatures be kept under control, for certainly they would not be totally eliminated.

When threshing finished, the business of dismantling the equipment - sheeting it up and getting it out and on the way to the next farm - was rapidly pursued. In short winter days, often the last sight of the departing outfit would be its dim outline, the glow from the engine's ash-tray, and a crazily swinging hurricane lantern attached to the last implement on tow.

The subject of steam engines as a source of power is not complete without mention of the 'portable' engine, which presumably was given that name since it represented the first type of steam-raising unit which could be moved from place to place by road, to provide power.

Its use to farming was mainly confined to driving threshing machines, and a farmer had to provide a team or teams of horses to haul both the 'portable' and the threshing 'box' from or to the farm premises.

Probably this was the very beginning of horse replacement

on farms and it could be argued that horses, thus, helped in their own departure from the agricultural scene.

It is possible, too, that politics had something to do with the slower development of the self-propelled steam engine for road use. The railway engine was already accepted as useful and safe because it ran on a laid track and encountered no other form of traffic. No such assurance was forthcoming for a road engine; therefore designers had to be content with producing a boiler on wheels until the law became more favourable.

I did not have the pleasure of seeing a portable engine driving a threshing box, but I clearly remember two units coming to some nearby woods where they were set up to drive saw mills, which reduced trees to planks on the site. Among the first tasks on this occasion was the sawing of sufficient planks to build sheds for their own coverage, and for open-sided sheds for sheltering the long saw benches.

Real traction engines were, therefore, a later development and of course were used for many and varied purposes because they were powerful and versatile in that they could be used both for haulage and for stationary driving. Apart from threshing the traction engine was also used for ploughing, which required the presence of two engines, but they were only effective in large and reasonably flat fields.

Ploughing engines were considerably larger than ordinary engines and were fitted with a large wire rope haulage drum, capable of holding possibly a mile of rope.

The drum was underslung between front and rear wheels, mounted horizontally for reasonable ground clearance.

For ploughing the engines were positioned on opposite sides of the field or patch with the rope from each engine shackled to a multi-furrow plough. As one engine hauled in, the other engine paid out, so that the plough shuttled back and forth between the two, and each trip resulted in some eight or ten furrows being turned, under the supervision of the man riding the plough.

The man's main responsibility was to reverse the plough at each end, this bringing another set of plough shares into operation for the return trip. This plough was of fairly massive construction and was probably the forerunner of the now well-known 'one-way plough,' designed to plough a field starting from one side and progressing across to the other, with all furrows being turned the same way.

When steam-ploughing, it was, of course, necessary to move each engine forward in turn, the exact distance necessary to bring it in line for the return haul; thus each engine moved when it was paying out rope.

Perhaps the largest traction engine of all was one built for a local firm of timber merchants, to haul out trees and load them onto timber waggons, and then to hitch up and take the massive load many miles to the firm's saw-mills. One of its main features was a large jib-crane fixed to the front of the engine and used to lift and place trees onto the timber carriages. For its period it was quite a masterpiece and well able to remove timber from the most awkward places. I knew the driver of this particular engine, which was the only one of its type ever built, and often marvelled at the dexterity with which he manipulated it in awkward places.

It is worth recording that horses were, in those days, very often averse to steam engines of any description and it was the self-imposed duty of every roadside farmer to provide some kind of adequate screening for the engine, often with the aid of rick sheets or cart sheets. Some horses would absolutely refuse to pass a steam engine under any circumstances, while others would only be persuaded to pass if they were led, so that quite a few generations were necessary before a breed evolved not afraid or cars or engines.

Great care was always taken of farm horses, and the waggoners were held responsible for their team's conditions and performance.

Until the advent of the agricultural tractor, the entire speed of all farm work was regulated by the walking pace of the horse; therefore the farmers had to ensure that horse teams were efficient working units, all the year round. Although some work was done by single horses, the bulk of farm work was done by teams, so that the same horses were kept together as much as possible, either in twos, threes or occasionally fours.

Their stabling was always good, well-cleaned and cozy, and in winter they were kept in permanently at night, which meant that waggoners had the additional task of feeding and grooming their charges, daily. Horses could winter out, but were invariably sluggish and unkempt and the unpleasant task of getting them in each morning, in all kinds of weather, was not a good way to start a day's work. With stabling, however, it was possible to keep teams in high fettle and 'full of work' as they used to say.

I spent many a pleasant half-hour in our stable, with its smell of Stockholm tar - used to dress horses' hooves when infected with 'thrush' (an itching complaint) and the aromatic smell of Neat's foot oil, used for preserving harness.

Here I watched them being fed and groomed after a heavy day in the fields. All sweat and mud was removed, and each horse made comfortable before having its main meal. They were not allowed much water until they had cooled down, since a horse would easily develop colic with attendant complications. Needless to say, the waggoner cared for his team before he himself thought of sitting down to his own meal.

The early moring grooming also took place before the waggoner had his own breakfast, and while the horses had theirs. This task could take anything up to an hour, and when it was finished the waggoner went into breakfast while the horses finished feeding. It was the custom to be 'hooking-to' in the fields by 8 am, or 7.30 am if light enough.

In the stable at night the quiet would only be disturbed by the steady and contented champ of masticating jaws, an occasional snort or pruffle, a resonant rasping noise as a halter chain was snatched through its retaining ring which was secured to the front board of the manger, and the clab of a hoof against the flooring. All this could be appreciated under the kindly light from the flickering hurricane lamp, a light which cast, seemingly, monster shadows of the horses and reflected off the many brasses on the harness hanging behind each horse. Hurricane lamps were the safest form of light for use around farm premises and were always hung up in a safe place in any building.

On very hot summer evenings, and when I was in my early teens, I would occasionally take a hip bath into an empty stall in the stable, having first put plenty of clean straw around, and set the bath on a horse blanket in the middle. My younger brother, in a mischievous mood, set up a bucket of cold water near a knot-hole in the loft above, after having arranged a trip mechanism actuated by a length of rope from the granary. When he judged my ablutions were nearly finished, he pulled, and down came a deluge, bringing with it hay and other weed seeds. The resultant gasping for breath and howls of laughter together with the sound of pounding feet on the granary steps as the culprit made his timely getaway, have provided many an evening of reminiscence and hearty laughter in our later years.

The milking herd had quite an important place on a mixed farm and was generally there both for providing milk and for replenishment of stock for beef production.

The milk was converted into either cheese or butter. In the case of cheese production, it was possible to even tell the farm of origin. The public had a far wider choice of cheese from which to make their selection, and the fat content generally controlled the price.

My recollections are of butter making, since we did not produce cheese in any quantity. Before the advent of the cream separator, the method of taking the cream from the milk was by tediously panning-out milk in shallow vessels, to allow the cream to rise. Dairies had to be large enough to permit an array of these pans to be spaced out from each miling. Cream, rising to the top, was skimmed off with a skimming dish and retained in earthenware steins, until churning day.

After the introduction of the labour saving cream separator I have spent many an hour steadily turning the handle to maintain the correct revolutions of the centrifugal mechanism upon which the machine functioned.

This speed was usually determined by listening for the correct humming sound, and came automatically after a little practice. Afterwards it was only a matter of watching the thin stream of cream issue from one spout and the full flow of separated milk from the other. As each pail became full it was carried up from the dairy and stood outside the door on the stones of the causey to await being emptied into the stone pig-swill cisterns. This was the opportunity for the farm cats to help themselves to the still warm froth and very soon each one would display a little white nose or beard, or both.

The weekly butter making operations involved considerable work and preparation, and all utensils had to be scrupulously cleaned before work started. Then the cream was prepared by addition of saltpetre and also colouring matter when the cows were living mainly on a root diet in winter - milk from cows feeding on fresh grass produces a naturally yellow butter.

Cream temperature was vital to easy butter making, and to check this a special floating thermometer, not unlike a hydrometer, was used.

When once started, churning had to be continued without pause until butter was produced. Results were best achieved by maintaining a slow, steady rotation, which eventually produced a noticeable thickening of the contents, to be followed by complete separation of the liquid and solid matter, the solids being butter in very small particles.

Continued rotation would gather these small particles into larger masses when it became necessary to rotate the churn in jerks, allowing the butter to fall from beater to beater inside, eventually making one or two large, shapeless masses wallowing in the residual buttermilk.

The butter would be removed at this stage and placed in a shallow vessel, known as a 'butter mit,' where it was kneaded and worked to remove all the remaining buttermilk before being made up into pound and half-pound rolls. In summer a certain quantity of the surplus butter would be salted and 'put down' in jars or basins for winter use.

The skim milk left behind after the cream was removed was principally fed to the pigs and to young calves when fed from the bucket, but local people would sometimes ask for it, since it still contained a small percentage of butterfat, and would help out where families were large. Buttermilk was also fed to the pigs, but it could be used in the house, either as a salad dressing or as a hot weather drink.

The calving period was, normally, early spring, and calves born during this time would be bucket-fed from a very early age. Their diet after the first few days would consist of fresh milk diluted with a certain amount of skim milk. After a month or so the fresh milk would be replaced by an addition of linseed meal or a prepared calf meal.

All these youngsters were kept together in a small loose-box type of place, known as the 'calf kit.' Before each meal they would be fastened up along a line of iron hurdles, with miniature tie-chains, with the object of keeping them under control and of accustoming them to being tied. Even so, feeding buckets were often sent flying by a lusty and ill-timed 'bunt.' The aroma coming from within a calf kit was probably the worst part of calf rearing. It clung to clothing so that many a "Phew!" was uttered and nose wrinkled when the wearer entered the house.

When the day came to turn the calves out to grass for the first time and they were allowed their first hesitant glimpse of the big outside, care had to be taken to ensure that they did not do themselves serious damage in their subsequent wild cavortings. I well remember one calf propelling himself at great speed through a thick holly bush, and his look of foolish surprise when he emerged on the other side was worthy of some cartoonist's pen.

A BARREL CHURN
B END OVER END CHURN
C TUB CHURN
D BUTTER MIT

3

BROADER PICTURES

Into my heart an air that kills
From yon far country blows:
What are those blue remembered hills,
What spires, what farms are those?

A.E.Housman

In addition to keeping a dairy herd, a substantial number of bullocks were raised from calves to be fattened up at either two or three years old. During the period of fattening they were shut up in loose boxes, or stock yards, thus performing the highly important task of producing large quantities of excellent manure. In fact, manure so produced was almost as valuable as the animals themselves - a value recognised by the fact that it often featured in tenancy agreements and could not be sold or transferred from one farm to another.

To feed bullocks three times a day, large quantities of pulped roots, either turnips or mangols, were prepared and subsequently mixed with other processed grains such as kibbled oats, maize meal, bran and selected cattle cake (linseed). The whole mixture smelled fit for human consumption.

On occasion, during the fattening period, it was necessary to 'mixen out' (clean out) these animals, and it was quite a thrill for me to stand safely behind a gate and watch the antics of such large beasts as they capered about during their short periods of freedom. However, even this welcome hour or so of liberty seemed not precious enough to be prolonged, for they could invariably be enticed back inside quite quickly at the sight of more food.

During the winter months home-grown corn was taken regularly to the mill to be ground into cattle food. The method of payment for this service was ages old and entailed the miller taking a fixed or agreed weight of corn from each bag to be ground.

On suitable days I was allowed to travel to the mill, either on the top of, or cozily ensconced among, the load of sacks, dependent on the weather.

While unloading or re-loading was in progress I would wander around and about the old black and white mill, peering curiously into this and that. One minute I would be watching the turbulent water of the mill race; the next, watching flotillas of ducks on the mill dam or the occasional ripple as a fish betrayed its presence in the still water of the dam.

Inside the mill one could feel the powerful vibrations of the grinding stones as they steadily reduced the grain to flour or meal. Through an opening at floor level could be seen a small portion of the massive undershot wheel which provided cheap power. Occasionally the miller would make us a present of an eel or two, which he scooped up out of an eel trap permanently built in the mill dam. These lively creatures would be put in a sound sack and tied up tightly to prevent their escape, and then carried home for supper.

Cattle to be sold had to make the journey to the nearest auction on foot, and in many instances this journey would have to start very early in the morning on account of the distance which had to be travelled. Fat cattle could only amble along very slowly after the first mile or so, and would flop down exhausted upon arrival.

Pigs and calves were usually transported in either a cart, lorry, waggon or float according to the number involved. These vehicles were temporatily fitted with side fencing known as 'rippling,' thus in effect making a pen on wheels, and for a load of pigs additional precautions would be taken in the form of a strong net, tied securely over the top of the vehicle.

A cow and calf for sale would usually mean the calf travelling in a cart or 'float,' with its mother walking concernedly behind.

When my school days started it was a common sight to meet droves of cattle or flocks of sheep on the road and if, by chance, two flocks of sheep met on the road, one flock would have to be turned into the nearest suitable field, while the other flock passed by.

Quite often animals on the move would be in the charge of professional drovers, rough looking characters as a rule, who always had one or two useful dogs working the flock along.

Farmers travelled in various types of vehicle - those who could afford it owned a special high trap with smart trappings and a spanking horse to go with it. The vehicles had rubber-shod wheels and were well sprung, while the coachwork was the best example of the coachbuilder's art, custom-lined and highly varnished.

Metal work was ornamented and polished and the whole rig set off by two large brass trap lamps and a long pliant whip, rhythmically nodding to and fro in its socket, beside the driver. Such vehicles were almost soundless when moving, and apart from the brisk clip of the horse's hooves on the road, the only other sound came from the low whirring of the revolving wheel spokes, when driven at speed. Others would favour a less attractive turn-out in the form of a 'tub' or 'float.'

Travelling by night was somewhat curious, since the side lamps, being situated fairly high up, cast a shadow of the horse directly ahead, which meant that he did not take kindly to pulling such a vehicle at night, and because of this had to be gradually accustomed to it.

Drivers of traps and other such vehicles had always to bear in mind the dangers which could quickly develop should their horse or pony take fright at some object or happening on the road.

Other light vehicles consisted of the very common high trap or 'shandray' and the ubiquitous float, which was used for a multitude of jobs on or off the farm.

Inns and hostelries were always well patronised by visiting farmers on market days on account of the stable accommodation offered. The yards at the rear would be full of parked vehicles of every variety and size, while the horses would be comfortably stabled and looked after by a paid ostler. Advertising of such accommodation was not necessary. Patronage was added to or lost by word of mouth. Casual conversation between farmers usually included an enquiry such as "Where do you.." or "Where does so and so put up?" and the answer "The Plough," or "The Dun Cow," usually led the enquirer to try out the facilities offered.

For those farmers who did not intend staying long at market, there was usually someone to be found to 'mind horse' on payment of a few coppers and certain characters were always to be seen hanging around the market prepared to undertake such light responsibilites.

Children on the roads to and from school were often given a lift in passing traps or carts. If we boys didn't get a lift we would run behind, hanging onto a rear fitting, a strap or chain.

All my early schooling was obtained by walking almost three miles each way to the village school, and, in those days, roads were surfaced with untarred stone, the settling medium being simply the wayside soil. Ruts and pot-holes were quite common and during wet weather such depressions would fill with muddy water. Pedestrians quickly found it necessary to avoid such places when the very occasional car passed, since mud and dirty water was spattered profusely by these and the odd - solid-tyred - motor lorry.

Conversely, in dry summer weather, these same surfaces were a mass of fine whitish dust, like flour, and if no rain fell road margins and hedges soon became covered. Motor vehicles raised voluminous clouds of this dust which could be seen from afar long before the vehicle itself came into view, and when two such mechanised monsters passed each other it was eqivalent to driving in a bad fog and equally dangerous, when visibility became virtually nil for a while.

We children plodded our way under these conditions daily, wet or fine, and yet, on looking back, I consider it did us no harm. We had a lot of good fun, and depending on the time of year certain activities would be in vogue, which seemed to make the distance traversed so much shorter.

February and March would see hoops (bowlers) in use by nearly everyone, and this would be followed by top spinning, when it was the ambition of every child to possess what was known as a 'flyer,' this being a top which would be whipped a long distance and still come down spinning.

Marble season usually followed and would last until May, when most games ceased until late September and October when 'conker' contests would finish off the season.

During spring our energies were directed towards bird-nesting; some had the idea of making an egg collection, while others were more inclined towards taking the eggs to eat, that is the eggs of moorhen and lapwing.

Naturally, the length of time it took us to get home after school was considerably extended because of deviations to well known ponds and pools, quartering of fields looking for lapwings' eggs, and, not least, tree climbing. Clothes had a very testing time, as a result of tree climbing, and my pockets were usually the receptacles of catapult ammunition, which convinced local animal and bird life to keep well out of range along the route.

As may be expected, we long distance school children were not exactly angels, and consequently were often in and out of trouble, mainly on our way home from school when time was less pressing. Fruit orchards were always an attraction, along with wayside plum and walnut trees.

It seems that we could never pass a wasps' nest without throwing stones and sticks at it, thus thoroughly rousing them up and making things unpleasant for the next passer-by.

I well remember the heavily laden crab-apple tree into which several of us threw stones just as an old open tourer-type car passed beneath. Being fully ripe, the crab-apples fell in hundreds so that the car was litarally swamped, even to some lodging in the driver's trilby hat. Needless to say, the car pulled up and the driver rounded on those who had not thrown anything. The real culprits had shot through the hedge and were lying low in the long grass.

NO GAPS IN THIS HEDGE

On another occasion two of us were caught dismantling a newly repaired gap in a roadside hedge, the farmer's stockman having effected the repair only that day. Having caught us in the act he marched us off to the farmhouse some distance away off the road. Since it was market day and the farmer and his wife had not yet returned, the stockman left us at the back door in the custody of his Old English sheep dog, whom he instructed laconically to "Watch 'em!" Eventually the farmer and his wife returned in their high trap and the stockman had a few words to say; as a result of this chat, the farmer warned us very firmly not to do such a thing again, and to get off home as quickly as we could; otherwise he would have "great pleasure in introducing his shoemaker to our behinds!"

Another pastime on the way home was for one boy to be the waggoner of two or three other boys, coupled together abreast with string tying their arms. The guide rein was tied to the outer arms on each team so that the youthful waggoner had control, or should I say was supposed to have control, because in a very realistic manner the team would behave exactly like high mettled horses, prancing, kicking, backing and edging sideways.

All this called forth the skill of the waggoner and his knowledge of a waggoner's words of command, but it broke the monotony of the long journey home, although I doubt whether it reduced the distance or conserved footwear.

Some children were harder on their clothes than others. Boots, in particular, had to be good quality, otherwise they would not be watertight. There were no such things as gum boots and Wellington boots in those days. Some parents got around this recurring expense by fitting their children out with clogs for the winter months, and this type of footwear had some distinct advantages, such as warmth in cold weather, and was very useful to slide over frozen puddles, or wayside ponds, and they were also cheap. They did, however, have one drawback; clogs were poor for use in snow, since it tended to build up into hard cakes between the clog irons, making walking difficult.

Mention must be made of the actual school facilities provided for children of the period and, in this respect, the locality was well provided for, there being three in the village in the form of or an infant school and separate schools for boys and girls.

I recall that the infant school was provided with a gallery at one end so that it resembled a lecture theatre in miniature. This was used for the toddlers, presumably because it was easier for the junior mistress to keep an eye on them.

Teaching was of a relatively high standard and the heads of each establishment spent virtually a lifetime of devoted service to their charges - this in classroom conditions which left much to be desired if measured alongside modern school requirements.

Pupil population in the boys' school fluctuated between ninety and one hundred and twenty, divided into six 'standards' and was shared between the headmaster and one lady assistant teacher.

Credit should be given to the local education authority of the time for putting sufficient emphasis upon the subjects of the three Rs (reading, writing and arithmetic). Other subjects were by no means neglected but they were never allowed to overshadow the three essentials. Thus it was that children at the end of their formal education were at least provided with the essential tools to expand their education and field of knowledge, at any time in later life.

The schools produced many bright pupils, but the number of Grammar school free places was limited and many parents could not afford to pay. Nevertheless, the basic foundation was well and truly laid for those who had the will or opportunity to build.

Here mention should be made of the volunteer fire brigade. The village and surrounding districts were well provided for in the shape of a horse-drawn 'Merryweather' fire engine of the manual beam-pump type. Firemen were recruited from within the village, preferably from those living reasonably near the fire station or engine house. In the event of a fire someone had to dash to the Parish Church and toll the big bell to call the brigade together, two of whom had the task of collecting a pair of horses on their way.

Horses were more of a problem than the men at times, especially in summer when out to grass. In this respect we schoolboys helped, or thought we helped, in rounding them up. Finding horses at night was problematical even by moonlight, so much so that on one occasion a searcher succeeded in haltering a cow.

We were usually allowed out of school to watch the fire brigade turn out for daytime fire alarms. On one occasion the outbreak was at a nearby corn mill and the road to it was mainly downhill. No horses being immediately available the men decided to run the engine the half mile or so with two of them manning the draught pole to steer. As it passed the school some of the older boys hopped over the playground wall to help push, with dire results. The heavy engine became unmanageable around a sharp bend and ran into the hedgebank, breaking the draught pole, thus delaying its arrival considerably. This lent further credence to the time-honoured remarks about having to add more fuel to keep the fire going in case it was out before the arrival of the brigade.

Perhaps the most priceless incident was the occasion when horses were at long last to be dispensed with and the engine in future towed to fires behind a Model T Ford, the property of the village publican, himself a very keen member of the brigade.

With the necessary towing attachment fitted, arrangements were made for a practice drill, the date being made known but not the time. During mid-day opening hours in the public house, a small party of resident American tourists heard about the new innovation in fire fighting and the part the landlord played, so they managed to distract his attention long enough for one of them to tamper with the engine. When the fire alarm did sound, out shot our enthusiastic publican to crank up his trusty steed, without any success. Up went the bonnet, andmore frantic cranking, far, far, faster than the tolling bell at the church. Minutes ticked by; the language became rosy and then definitely ruddy as other members of the brigade strolled up to enquire or offer ill-timed suggestions. To add to this uproar, were the remarks of the Americans who had been watching from an upstairs window until, red in the face and stuck for words, our would-be Jehu had slammed his bonnet down in disgust, only to hear a voice from above saying that the plug leads were crossed...pandemonium!

4

WORK AND PLAY

This is the land of lost content,
I see it shining plain,
The happy highways where I went
And cannot come again.

A.E.Housman

Introduction to farm work was quite a gradual process, but from the age of ten I found myself doing all kinds of odd jobs, for some of which I was paid a few pennies when Saturday came round.

I was never driven to do work - rather more often encouraged by being shown a good example and the correct and easiest way to use a particular tool. My father impressed on me that, no matter what the job, it was worth doing well, and that the correct and skilled use of tools or implements was half the battle.

On looking back it seems that I was regularly picking up snippets of knowledge to do with the various aspects of farm-work.

Such a thing as the correct way to insert a pitchfork into a pile of loose straw or 'cock' of hay, which, for the uninformed, is to stick the fork well down into the half furthest away from the operator. By doing this it is easy to pick up cleanly and also avoid loose material falling over the wielder's head.

Sheaves or 'shoffs' of corn were always pitched with their ear-ends towards the loader or rick builder, and as near as possible to hand so that he would not have to reach far for them.

A corn sheaf had to be tied in one certain manner, by hand, with a 'bond' of loose straw, the end of which was given a deft twist and a quick tuck-under to make it secure for reasonable handling.

When hedge and other trimmings were being burnt, the

kindling was always done from the leeward side so that combustion had to progress against the wind. This ensured that everything was burned, and did not produce a quick flame-up which would have consumed just the lighter material only.

Corn sacks were tied in a particular fashion by first ensuring that the empty sack space at the top was tightly gathered in, so as to prevent undue movement of the contents during subsequent handling.

Handling sacks of grain or other produce was made much easier if one was shown the 'knack,' and to this end I was taught to do everything as handily as possible and to conform to the same standard, in this respect, as other workmen.

By easy stages I was taught to milk by hand, always being given a cow which was quiet and an easy milker. I can also remember the feeling of pride when I successfully completed the hoeing of my first ridge row of turnips, right across the field.

Farm life, of course, was not all work and no play; we children enjoyed many carefree hours - more so during the longer days of summer.

Great fun came our way when all the harvest was safely in the rickyard, after which we could play hide-and seek and make 'hides' by crawling in between the close-set ricks. Our favourite time for this game was when the ricks cast ghostly shadows and the bats were flying around, a setting which produced the msot delicious and tingling shivers up our youthful spines.

When I was a little older I took to climbing Hopton Hill, the steep hill feature which rose quite abruptly a little distance to the north of the farmstead. Here among the rock formations near the summit I would find numerous jackdaws' nests, and in one place a peculiar small cave-like recess, where I could sit and enjoy the panoramic view below, stretching out in almost limitless distance to the horizon.

An extension of the hill complex was even more interesting, since it possessed a succession of vertical sandstone cliffs near the top. In fact the hill was almost horseshoe shaped and topped off with an artificial earthwork around its whole periphery. The closed area on the top was quite flat, of some nine or ten acres in extent, and under cultivation.

This was the site of a Roman military camp, and my visits there were always full of excitement because I found no difficulty in transporting myself in imagination back to those far-off days.

Sitting up there, high on the cool leafy shade and solitude,

I could clearly visualise the camp activity - legionaries going about their many camp tasks in the safety of such a magnificent stronghold, while bands of woad-painted Britons lurked about far below in the, then, untamed countryside.

This rock fastness was the abode of thousands of jackdaws, some of their nests entirely filling narrow clefts for a height of fifteen to twenty feet, indicating years of successive building. I usually timed one of my visits to coincide with the time young jackdaws were about to leave their nests, so that for some years I always had one or two tame birds at home. Everyone seemed to enjoy their funny ways, but of course they became too tame, and eventually fell prey to the farm cats, quite often to the relief of my mother because of their thievish habits.

An instance of this acquisitiveness comes to mind, when one of these pets was surprised in full flight from the dairy-cum-larder with a large three-cornered slice of jam tart in his beak. On this occasion he lost his rations because of my mother's quick reaction and dexterity with the mop head she was carrying at the time.

Playtime done I seemed to find an interest in most jobs about the farm and I suppose harvest times provided most of them, especially the corn harvest.

At first I was a kind of errand boy, which entailed making journeys to and from the harvest field carrying the beer crocks and lunch baskets. The bottles were made of glazed earthenware and were wicker-wound for protection, and I carried one in each hand, to ensure balance. When the bottles were filled from the cellar the especially strung corks were pushed well home, and a solemn warning given to me not to shake the crocks unduly, but needless to say I occasionally couldn't resist giving a shake now and again just for the pleasure of hearing the bang as the cork flew out. The thirsty harvesters could quickly determine what had happened.

Corn in our part of the country was cut by the reaper, and later with the self-binder by driving around the field from the outside towards the centre. Most of the fields were four-sided. If not, this was rectified after a few rounds, and gradually the square of standing corn would grow smaller and smaller.

The most interesting part of the day came when the standing corn was reduced to a small patch in the middle of the field. This was the time when rabbits and hares who had been withdrawing from the reaping blade discovered that the cover was too small to contain them, and would bolt for fresh and safer

TYPICAL WELL BUILT LOAD OF CORN

surroundings. All the harvesters took a hand in their destruction and any weapons to hand were used to this end. Guns sticks, stones and dogs were employed in an effort to reduce their numbers. Rabbit burrows would be dug out afterwards, and it was not uncommon to find those near the centre of the field with anything from ten to thirty occupants, some suffocated by their numbers.

The result of harvesting operations on many farms produced a glut of rabbits, so much so that conveying them to market and the occupation of a kerbside stand were not worth the effort, since it was another instance of supply exceeding demand. Furthermore there was no refrigeration in those days and consequently rabbits would not remain fresh for very long in the warm weather of harvest.

With the carrying home of the harvest, there was always fun to be had riding in the harvest carts or waggons, or in the job of 'leading horse' as the vehicle was moved stage by stage along the row of 'mows' or stooks.

I was soon to find out that the horses obeyed quite an unusual word of command when doing this work. This word was an abbreviated form of "hold you," and as such really meant to warn those up on the load that a move was about to be made. It is doubtful whether a horse would have understood the full pronunciation, however, since the words were always shortened to "Owd-ya."

Horses were taught to respond to certain words when they were broken in, and a good horse team could, virtually, be controlled by word of mouth. This was necessary when two, three or four animals were harnessed in chains and followed behind each other. The shaft horse, or horse hooked to the implement or vehicle, was always specially selected for intelligence and obedience.

While still quite small I spent many happy hours in plough fields where I was permitted to walk behind the plough holding the 'plough tails' or handles, with the actual ploughman walking at the side holding the reins, ready to take over at the end of a furrow to 'throw the plough out,' and 'set it in' again after turning.

If I was there when ploughing finished for the day (unhooking) I usually had a ride on one of the horses back to the stable. It was noticeable that when returning from the field the horses would be in quite a hurry, so much so that they would scarcely obey the word "Whoa" if it was necessary to stop for some reason or other.

This was quite a different matter on their way to the fields in the morning when they would only walk at half speed, and even the slightest word was readily misconstrued as "Whoa."

The lighter side of country life was taken care of during the summer months by the many village fêtes and flower shows, and small agricultural shows. These occasions were marked by a period of intense activity on the part of the organising bodies and no effort was spared to produce a pleasant afternoon's entertainment for both young and old.

My memories of local flower shows recall the importance of the weather, so that a bright sunny day would see whole families setting out. Clad in their best suits and dresses, they would head towards the show ground where groups of people intermingled, all of them chattering away to each other as if they had not met for years, and perhaps on the wind would come the sound of a brass or silver band engaged to provide the afternoon's musical entertainment.

These events were usually held in the grounds of the local Hall, or Manor, where they took advantage of the layout of lawns and gardens, and included everything in the way of entertainment and amusement. There would be competitive displays of fruit, flowers and vegetables, laid out attractively on wooden tresles inside large marquees, whilst outdoors there were foot races, cycle races - both slow and fast - obstacle races, pony rides, Punch and Judy shows, skittles and bowling for a pig. The eventual winner of the pig would, upon being presented with the noisy little fellow, be subjected to a battery of comment, including such remarks as "I'll 'ave my bit of pork for Christmas," or "I dunna like too much fat with my bit of pork, mind."

Most of the afternoon would be taken up in judging the various competitions and the sports programme would keep officials running hither and thither for even longer.

The band would play popular tunes. Old people would sit and chat with more distant friends. Youngsters would be playing around, getting themselves lost and found. Everyone enjoyed everyone else's company equally - landlord, farmer and workman, but there was always that friendly measure of respect between land owner and tenant farmer, or between farmer and workman.

Towards evening the lawns would be cleared for dancing - dancing on delightfully close-cut grass, perhaps by the light of the rising moon.

For a little boy, the end of a perfect day would be a tired but contented walk home, with the dance music growing fainter and fainter until finally it faded completely away on the night air.

This picture is not complete without a small additional reference to our village schools, which were Church schools maintained to some extent and partly administered by the village Squire and his family, who were interested in individual children - particularly their welfare and school attendances.

The Squire's lady made it a duty to call at the schools once every week to hear the register called. Many of the children had to walk long distances over poor roads, so that some arrived with wet feet. Because of this the Squire's family provided felt slippers in a variety of sizes, so that wet footwear could be taken off and dried, while children from poorer families were provided with footwear and coats or cloaks.

To mark the occasion of the Squire's birthday, an event called 'The Lawn Treat' would take place when all children were given an afternoon off from school to attend. For this event it was a requirement that all pupils should parade with a large posy of wild flowers carefully tied to one end of a four-foot willow stick, previously peeled so that it had dried out white. These were carried rifle fashion on the shoulder and, headed by the village band, the whole assemble marched off in column to a lawn near the Hall to take part in an afternoon of games and races, the winners of events being given small money prizes.

At the end of the afternoon's entertainment a bumper tea was provided in a large marquee and the Squire accorded three cheers to mark yet another birthday.

5

COMMON FOLK

Ale that the Ploughman's heart up keeps
    And equals it with Tyrants' thrones
That wipes the eye that over weeps
    And lulls in dainty and sure sleep
        His wearied bones.

Old Song - 'In praise of ale'

It was perhaps fortunate, because of the wealth of good will and helpful neighbourliness, that our farm was situated in a locality which, in earlier times, had featured two or three areas of common or heath land.

Part of the farm was, in fact, old common land and accordingly not very fertile unless farmed with respect and with liberal visitations from the 'muck cart.'

Many of our near neighbours were the occupants of the familiar small holdings which had been literally carved out of waste land by their forbears, and which had suffered enclosure by, and in, the surrounding estates of the period. The enclosures took place over a period of time in the latter part of the 17th Century and early and middle 18th Century.

It seems that, though it may have been discussed at Westminster, common land enclosures never were subject to a Parliamentary Act; therefore the latter enclosures, with which we are concerned, were illegal.

Land enclosure had been going on for hundreds of years, where each village had its patch or patches of ground for open farming, but this was not necessarily common land; in fact it would be good arable land.

Common land was another matter. It was poor, and probably infested with gorse and heather so that anyone who liked to take on the task of carving out a homestead was welcome to it. The common-dweller, having made some kind of show, neighbouring landlords (estates) saw that such areas could become a useful addition at no great cost.

Commoners did not rebel because a shilling a year rent and

possibly a new house, seemed a small price to pay.

In return for a small annual rent, the landlord pledged that these 'commin men,' as they were called, would receive such benefits as land drainage, repairs to property, and the construction of a few narrow roads or lanes.

Where the dwelling house was either too small or dilapidated, the local landowner would offer to build a new one. This, in fact, was often the case because common land houses were always built in a hurry and therefore quite small.

The estates, meanwhile, increased in size and value and also benefited by the elimination of tracts of free land which otherwise would have bisected their game preserves.

The original 'commin men' were relatively poor and hard working, but at least they were free men and they bred a race which set no mean value on this freedom. To this day, the families who can trace their ancestry back to these people still display a marked independence, and an unwillingness to be pushed around by any form of officialdom. The quality of their labour and the variety of their skills made these men much sought after for work on large neighbouring farms.

Common land was probably what we should now include among 'marginal land' (land only marginally fit for agriculture). As such it was of no interest and under an old law was designated common land and anyone who could start to build a dwelling on it and have smoke coming out of the chimney in one day, became a freehold commoner. Hence the hurry in building, and also the chimney being built first.

These chimneys were massive and often partially separated from the houses, which had thatched roofs - the addition of a few roughly built outhouses, enough for one or two cows and a horse together with a pig sty, completed the entire building.

When erecting these homes, all common dwellers made sure that a large copper was built in somewhere. This served a double purpose, being used for regular brewings of beer and on the occasions when pigs were killed.

When men were working on

BREW HOUSE AND BAKE HOUSE

these remote holdings, or away on some nearby farm, beer would be their sole liquid refreshment. No one thought of any other drink for the field. Presumably in the cider districts the same would apply.

As a boy I often worked with these 'commin men' and found myself always in good company, where even the heaviest task was made all the lighter because of individual handiness and good will.

In earlier days it was to be expected that the tenets of Wesleyanism should take easy root among such people, but it took the more radical and fiery doctrine of Primitive Methodism to rouse them to action and to building many little wayside chapels still to be found in country areas. This simple and direct faith must have struck many sympathetic chords among the earlier 'commin' dwellers, up and down the whole countryside, who, feeling the yoke of the landlords or estate holders, turned readily to the Primitive cause.

They would remember too that the illegal notices which gave effect to the enclosures, had been displayed upon the doors of their Parish Churches, and the reminder would serve to make them turn their backs upon churches generally and make their adherence to Primitive Methodism and their Chapels even more fervent.

Although I regularly attended Sunday School at the nearby Primitive Methodist Chapel, I was christened in our Parish Church, where my father was a member of the choir. Since the Parish Church was three miles away, it was more reasonable to attend Chapel Sunday School, but on summer evenings, and perhaps on a good moonlight night, I would walk to Church with my father, and sit beside him in the choir stalls.

Attending both Church and Chapel did not seem odd at that age, though there were differences. The formal Anglican liturgy contrasted with the more spontaneous utterances of Methodism, and sermons delivered by unlettered lay preachers were often made more wholesome by the use of rural terms and phrases.

Sometimes, when we came out of Church, we would accompany an old lady to her little black and white thatched cottage on our way home. Upon entering she would turn up her paraffin lamp, shake up the fire into a cheerful blaze and then produce biscuits and one of her many and various bottles of homemade wine. She would carefully pour out three glasses, but only about two fingers for me, which I thoroughly enjoyed at the time.

Upon bidding the lady, who I gathered was a distant member of the family, goodnight my father would set off at a brisk pace for home, but oh! that first mile or so....my little legs were not used to strong drink and I would willingly have subsided into the ditch for a nap.

However, some hidden force kept me going until the effects wore off and I did not tell my father of my predicament - would it be for fear my ration would be cut?

The Chapel's year was outlined in a special folder called 'THE PLAN' which gave notice of the name of the preacher who would take the service each Sunday, at each Chapel in the circuit. One or two of these local preachers were known for their lengthy sermons and it was public knowledge that on one occasion one of these long-winded preachers locked his congregation in, having had previous experience when some youths seated at the back had walked out before the end of the service. Taking the key with him into the rostrum he declared in a loud and firm voice, "Now you're here, you've got to have it."

It is also on record that another local preacher on the circuit, getting a little carried away during the delivery of his sermon, exhorted his congregation with these words: "My friends, let us all have another pull at the heavenly barrel, it 'inna' (isn't) dry yet."

Perhaps it was this down-to-earth faith which drew the people, and no doubt it accorded well with the mood of the 'commin' dwellers and perhaps provided the one bright star in an apparently darkened sky.

These people of the 'commins' had been brought up to accept adversity with resolution and they were always willing to help one another or to pull together in matters of work. This amicable association of the soil must surely be a relic of remote antiquity and noted by Xenophon where, in his 'Oeconomicus,' he makes Socrates inform Critobulus that the earth taught men kindliness - because on a farm one had to be prepared and willing to lend a hand to one's fellow men.

Examples of the 'commin man's' native wit and mode of expression were delightful to hear and one instance of this comes to my mind. A funeral had taken place at the Parish Church. The rector, of some twenty years' standing, after officiating at the internment, was saying a few words to some of the mourners, during which he spoke to an ancient 'commin man' who was very deaf. He had to repeat his words several times in order to be heard, and finally raising his voice said, "I'm surprised to hear that your holding is in our parish; I always thought it was in the adjoining one." Our ancient friend, having digested what was said, suddenly spoke up in that loud voice peculiar to some deaf people, saying, "Well, if I'd bin ploughin' in the same field for 20 years, I think I should 'a know'd all the corners by now."

It is not improbable that sayings such as 'as bad tempered as a toad under a set of harrows,' or a child said to be 'as busy as a dog in 'duff' (dough)' originated in common land localities, and a little thought and imagination readily proves how descriptive and apt these sayings are.

With the march of time, these scattered yet closely associated communities are losing their identity and individuality. Whole families have left and strangers have moved in. The 'commin' type houses with their curious chimneys have been knocked down to make room for modern dwellings, and newcomers have bought up plots of land to develop where one used to find 'crafts' or crofts.

The little chapels are finding it hard to keep open. Some are indeed closed already and regretfully one must face the fact that, apart from place names and a few family names, there is little to remind one of former times.

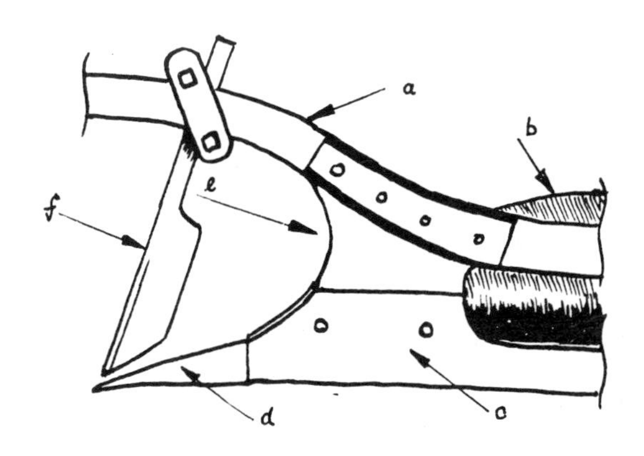

THE SINGLE FURROW PLOUGH

a	Plough beam	d	Plough share
b	Mould board	e	Plough throat
c	Land side plate	f	Coulter

6

SEASONAL ARTS AND SKILLS

Who can live in heart so glad
    As the merry country lad!
Who, upon a fair green baulk,
    May, at pleasure, sit and walk;
And, amid the azure skies
    See the morning sun arise!

Nicholas Breton

To the uninitiated, the annual round of farm work might seem to be divided into seasonal group activities, but this is only partially true because the art of good cultivation and stock raising requires long term planning and preparation.

To do this effectively and in order to harvest a certain crop or to market certain animals, the initial moves must be made one, two, or perhaps even three, years in advance.

Growing older my interests were taken up more and more by the fundamentals of farming, and with all this overlapping of activities, I found some difficulty in deciding whether the farming year had any beginning or ending.

It was, however, obvious that no task on a farm lasted very long - a few weeks at the most, and then something else would take priority, with little chance of anything becoming monotonous.

Many of the jobs could and did produce a real sense of satisfaction and pride of achievement, when completed, so that there was a healthy sense of competition among the men from different farms in their own specialities.

No waggoner would think of turning out with an untidy, ill-groomed team, while ploughing and ridging had to be of gun-barrel straightness. The hedger would only be satisfied with an example of his craft which would be 'fit to stun old Covington's hedge layer.' The rickmaker and thatcher would be similarly competitive and the net result of it all put a certain amount of pleasure into farm work generally.

Springtime was the season of greatest activity, with special effort being made to get all arable land ploughed and worked down into a good seed bed, either for spring sown corn, or for root crops.

Ploughing was a very specialised craft, with particular attention being paid to the depth necessary for the root system of the crop to follow, or the depth and type of subsoil.

A plough was also an implement for burying or digging in any manure spread upon the ground, and to do this certain additional tools had to be fitted, known as 'skelps.'

A good ploughman had to know how to set his plough for each operation and also to know the effect of sloping ground, stony ground and wet patches.

When I was big enough I was started off with a single-horse plough, my job being to 'peel' stubbles over after harvest. Later on I became proficient enough to manage two steady horses, and to plough the traditional straight furrow, but it was not until much later that I could draw a straight 'cop' and finish a straight 'reon.'

The sound made by the plough-share as it knifed its way through good solid turf is still with me. It could be compared to the continuous rub of sandpaper on wood, with an occasional rasp as a stone slid along the 'shell-board' or mould board, this being the thin, beautifully curved casting which turned the soil of the furrow over, laying it against the preceding one. The intermittent creaking of the whipple-trees and thud of hooves completed the sound picture.

To plough correctly was a skilled job and the handling of a team played an important part. Care had to be exercised at all times against such incidents as the horses taking fright, or getting their legs over the chains, occurrences which could easily develop into a first-class mix-up.

In all types of cultivation involving the use of horses the waggoner had to walk behind his implement and in this way he could readily note the need for any adjustment. When harrowing, for instance, it was possible to have the towing point wrongly located, which resulted in 'tines' following each other.

In a similar manner ploughs and 'scuffles' could be adjusted to tow in or out as required by adjusting the 'buck,' a simple device located at the point of attachment of the whipple trees. By selecting the right hole for the pin, an implement could be made to run to the left, right, or straight.

Walking behind a plough or some such implement for days at a time in all kinds of weather and on many different soil surfaces, was quite a task in itself. It was small wonder that

IN MY FATHER'S FOOTSTEPS

a waggoner developed a peculiar gait, which was probably the origin of the term 'hobbledehoy,' meaning a clumsy or awkward fellow. This method of walking represented the easiest gait to keep up all day on uneven surfaces, or in the furrow behind the plough.

Waggoners in general were a cheerful race, very competitive in the matter of team turnout, and often to be heard singing and whistling about their work, nor did long hours of work worry them unduly. A measure of his work, accepted by farmer and ploughman, was one acre per day if he were ploughing with a single plough, set some five to eight inches deep.

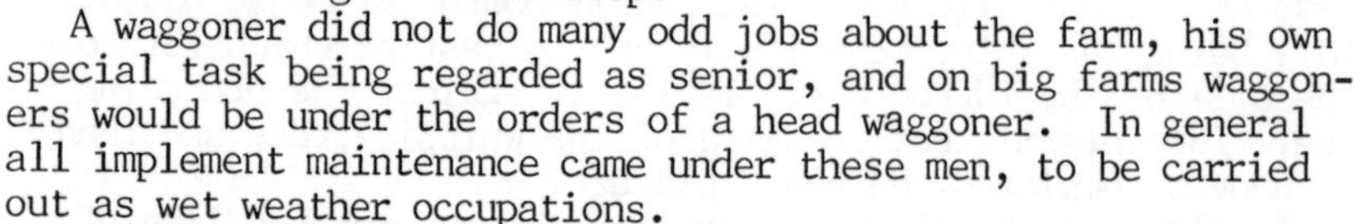

A waggoner did not do many odd jobs about the farm, his own special task being regarded as senior, and on big farms waggoners would be under the orders of a head waggoner. In general all implement maintenance came under these men, to be carried out as wet weather occupations.

Hard weather was the time for carrying the farmyard manure out into the fields and a time when stockyards, loose-boxes and sties were emptied of their aromatic contents. As a fertiliser its value was tremendous, since manure from corn-fed bullocks ranked very high on the scale, and in addition the straw matter would remain in the soil, steadily decomposing for periods up to and exceeding a year.

The spring sowing of corn was a task suited to the drier days of late February and March when good seed beds could be easily prepared. The task of sowing with a corn drill was not, in itself, very difficult. Provided the right train of gears was selected to sow the correct weight per acre, a man following the drill had only to see that the seed box was level when it was moving over hilly features and that all the seed sprouts were unobstructed and sowing.

The waggoner would probably have his team in chains - pulling one behind the other, and with usually only two horses, for this work; and his main concern would be to travel up and down the field in perfectly straight lines without 'baulking' a strip.

No waggoner liked a baulk, since his short-comings would be there for all to see in the growing crop, and good natured leg-pulling would surely be his lot for many a day to come when instead of corn growing there were patches of weeds.

The art of sowing by hand was far more difficult and was as old as time itself. This 'sowing broadcast' was an accomplishment not easily acquired; in fact, it seemed that there were less competent broadcast sowers than for any other job on a farm. Apart from being able to sow with either hand, a knowledge of seed qualities was vital, together with an almost nautical appreciation of the effects of wind.

Sacks of seed corn would be set across a field at convenient intervals, and in line with the direction of the wind, so that the broadcaster could travel from sack to sack on a fair filling of his seed hopper, which he carried almost chest-high and suspended from a strap, slung bandolier fashion.

The technique of sowing in this manner lay entirely in the co-ordination of movement between opposite arm and leg. The distributing sweep of the arm was timed to coincide with the forward movement of the opposite leg, a fresh supply of seed being taken from the hopper as the nearside foot made its passage forward.

This sequence would hold good for one direction and would be reversed on making the return crossing of the field, and had to become automatic, because strict attention had to be paid to the width being covered and to the necessary straight line of walk, in order not to over-sow patches, and not to leave 'baulks.' The old quotation 'as ye sow so shall ye reap,' was surely founded on the act of sowing rather than on the quality of seed and the seed bed.

I was taught to sow by more economic methods than distributing actual seed. My father started me off with hopperfuls of loose dry soil, and it took quite a long time to get the hang of it before being let loose with actual seeds.

The most difficult seed to sow was that of the small grass and clover mixtures. These were so infinitesimal that a single seed could hardly be seen and consequently they were affected by even the lightest breeze. Yet a good broadcaster on a favourable day could make an exceptionally fine job of seeding a field.

An improvemnet on this method of sowing fine seeds was provided by the small 'fiddle drill,' so called because its

THE ART OF SOWING BROADCAST
(Under-sowing spring corn with clover/rye grass seeds)

operation resembled the movement of a violin bow. There was also another implement called a 'seed barrow' which was wheeled along like a wheelbarrow, being a long trough-like affair, spanning approximately five yards.

The sowing of turnip and mangold crops was not very difficult, because the seed was drilled-in by a universal type of horse-drawn seed drill, on ground which had been previously ridged up - the implement sowing two ridges at a time. A waggoner had only to adjust the machine to sow the correct weight per acre and then to follow behind, ensuring that the delivery pipes or coulters were free from rubbish, as they cut their way along the truncated ridges.

Hoeing these crops commenced when the young plants were about one inch high, but before a start was made, a horse-drawn side hoe would be passed between the ridges to cut away surplus soil and the accompanying weed growth.

Hoeing served a twofold purpose, that of thinning out plants to the correct distances, and the removal of all remaining weeds, by simply pushing the surplus out to the space between each ridge or row. The art of hoeing really lay in doing it at speed, leaving well-spaced plants free from weeds of any description. The cleanliness of a man's work could be seen later, when weeds rapidly fouled the crop if left at hoeing time. (See drawing p 59)

Working in good conditions, a proficient workman could hoe an acre per day, but it would be a day of twelve or fourteen hours, commonly worked by men employed on a piecework basis at that time of the year.

As a boy I was not expected to move at speed, and to this end I was allowed out with a few ridges at one end of the field, with instructions to take my time and to make a good neat job. It took several seasons to work up to the required standard and speed, but I was allowed to hoe with the others after a time, starting off last and being helped along when I fell behind.

The ability to hoe with right or left hand leading on the hoe handle was also a final and welcome accomplishment, since the change of posture could give much relief, a crick in the neck being a common discomfort due to a fixed head position.

Main crop potatoes were planted at about the same period or a little earlier, on ground which had previously been well dressed with farmyard manure and, as with other crops, the ridging up of the ground was carried out very carefully with a ridge plough to ensure that width and depth were continuously maintained, whilst the standard of straightness usually conformed to Euclid's definition of a straight line. A variation was sometimes introduced by applying farmyard manure in between each ridge and the seed potatoes would be 'dropped' directly onto this rich deposit, and the covering of them was done by simply splitting each ridge with the same implement as that used for drawing up the original ridges.

At this time of year a very cosmopolitan variety of scarecrows could be seen in the fields. Some of them were very realistic, and others not so impressive, and in addition dead crows or rooks would swing, spreadeagled in the wind, as a grim warning to others of their kind. All birds, of course, were not regarded as harmful to farming and some of those which were only did damage under certain conditions - usually when crops were already pest afflicted.

Working in the fields in spring was always a pleasure if one cared to observe the activities of birds in the breeding season. Of these, I think the common plover or 'peewit' was one of the most interesting, and it was always worthwhile pausing to watch their aerobatic displays when the eggs or young chicks were about and the cockbirds very much in evidence.

At this time it was not uncommon for young rooks to be flying with their parents, and should a flock land on a field where peewits were nesting one could be sure of trouble, since both rooks and crows have a liking for eggs, and even for young chicks.

On such occasions all the adult peewits would take to the air in an attempt to drive off intruders. The aerobatics would be breath-taking, and their efforts so sustained that their objective would usually be attained, with the exception of, perhaps, one or two young rooks too afraid or too unsure of themselves to risk taking the air.

These unfortunates would be subjected to a firstclass exhibition of ground strafing, with peewits coming in so low and fast that the young rook or crow would have to squat low to avoid being cuffed by the flashing wings.

7

HAY HARVEST

Before the breeze the hayfields play,
So like the rolling main
Oh! make the very most of what
Will all too soon be lain.

A.B.Tinsley

The root fields occupied all available manpower until hay harvest time arrived, but the act of cutting a lush field of standing clover hay always seemed to me to be an act of sacrilege.

This valuable source of winter feed, although generally called hay, could, in fact, be either 'meadow hay' or 'clover hay' according to how and where it was grown.

If an ordinary permanent pasture was allowed to grow on in the spring, by keeping the cattle out, then the resultant grass crop would be meadow hay, and consist of all the grasses and clover (usually White Dutch) which composed the pasture.

It was the hay crop form these fields which produced, and still produces, the never-to-be-forgotten smell of 'new-mown hay.' Although all grasses give off some aroma as they gradually wither during the process of hay making, the real smell of new-mown hay is imparted by the relatively insignificant grass 'Sweet Vernal'.

The other source of fodder came from fields which had been seeded as one or perhaps two year leys, later to produce crops of clover hay consisting mainly of rye grasses, red clover and perhaps some vetches. On good land exceedingly heavy crops were common, and, although a somewhat coarser type of hay, it was very popular and also provided a useful break crop in the four-course farming system.

In addition to this the red clover, being one of the group of plants capable of fixing nitrogen in the soil, helped to increase soil fertility, so that when the field was ploughed and the next crop sown, it was expected to be a good one. To keep the four course system intact it was usual to follow with a cereal crop - generally wheat.

Hay cutting time, of course, meant the loss for another year of that most pleasant of all farming sights, the glorious wave forms gambolling endlessly across the sheen-like expanse of field, under the influence of frolicking winds and warmed by friendly sun, perhaps dappled occasionally by the shadow of a passing 'cotton wool' cloud.

The racket created by the mowing machines also disturbed that shy and rather rare bird, the cornrake or landrail, whose grating cry from the hidden recesses of the field had been so evident to the discerning ear, prior to cutting. This bird, related to the coot and moorhen but camouflaged like a partridge or ptarmigan, when disturbed, moved into other cornfields which would remain undisturbed for another two months.

Roads were never mown round clover and hay fields. Instead the first trip round would be about one mowing machine width in from the hedge. When the field was finished, that which remained standing round the outside was cut by making one or perhaps two circuits in the REVERSE direction.

Haymaking was simplified by inventions such as the horse-drawn 'swarth turner' or 'tedder.' Before the introduction of these implements all hay was turned by hand with the aid of long-handled hay rakes, made of wood (See page 15). A gang of men, using these, would move in echelon round and round a field, each one continuously turning one swath.

When dry enough - haymade - it would be got up into 'cocks' of approximately one good pitchfork or pikeful each, ready for carrying to the rick yard. Plenty of skill was also required to put a good load on a waggon or cart, while even more skill was necessary to constuct a well-shaped and waterproof rick.

To get the maximum load on a particular vehicle, special harvest gearing would be fitted, rather like outriggers, and the load would be built around these, in tiers. The loader had, in the case of a cart, to take special care not to make his load 'light on,' that is heavy at the rear, since severe out-of-balance in this direction could result in the strangulation of the horse in the shafts due to upward drag on the collar.

Men of long experience could tell when hay was fit to carry by the feel of it and also by the sound made when moving it. If it was crisp and produced a pleasant rustling sound, it was described as being in good 'fettle.'

Rick building was a job usually carried out by one man, who by his proven skill had established himself as the man for the

THE ART OF THATCHING

job. Briefly, his constructions had to withstand all kinds of wind and weather; they had to remain dry throughout and they had to look well. The golden rule in stack making lay in keeping the middle higher than the outsides during every stage of construction. This inclination towards the middle ensured that all rain falling either on the roof or driven by wind against the sides, drained off again. Ricks built with their centres lower than the outsides would be wet from roof to bottom, and the hay fit only for manure.

The finished rick would be carefully combed down all round with a hay rake, so as to leave all grass and clover stems inclined downwards, but it would not be thatched until it had sunk down to its consolidated level and the 'sweat' had finished.

Hay harvested, even in ideal conditions, would sweat, but anxiety only arose when, owing to poor harvest weather, damp material had been gathered in, because of the very considerable risk of fire, caused by spontaneous combustion.

Considerable ingenuity was called for to ventilate such ricks, vertical vent holes being formed by pulling a straw-filled filled sack or two up through the rick as its level rose, or perhaps inverted 'ship' (sheep) troughs would be laid across at different levels with their ends left protruding. Sometimes too, a course of wheat-straw battens would be laid across between every second load. The straw-filled sacks had to be large and well stuffed, to create a round chimney which acted as a ventilator shaft, helping to keep the rick cool.

The reason that wheat-straw battens were used, rather than any other kind, was that wheat-straw is very hard and does not compress so much as oats or barley straw; therefore it provides a measure of ventilation.

A critical rick is one which is seriously overheating and becoming a fire hazard, and had to be watched for temperature rise by inserting iron rods at various levels. If the heat was excessive the rods might be too hot to hold, and then the rick would be quickly pulled apart before a fire developed.

In a normal season any spare time between hay harvest and corn harvest was usually devoted to hedge brushing. The hedges were always kept in good order so that they served as an effective fence and provided a certain amount of shelter for animals.

A hedge, particularly hawthorn, which was regularly trimmed back to the previous level of cut, would, in time, acquire a 'set' or 'lay' so that subsequent trimming became more solid and twig ends inclined to the direction of cut.

At the same time all ditches were opened up by cutting out weed and grass growth. This being the time of lowest water, ditching was relatively easy and all obstructions such as soil from rabbit scratchings and mole digging, would be removed by means of a ditching tool known as a 'skippit,' a long-handled shovel with turned up sides. Hedging and ditching was generally reckoned to be done at the time when the annual growth had reached maximum, and when everything was 'sappy' and work less laborious.

The smell of newly withered hedge trimmings, especially after a shower of rain, is just another of the treasures of the countryside which she keeps to herself, or in reserve for the privileged few.

The task would be finished off by gathering all trimmings into regular heaps for removal to make rick bottoms, or for burning at a later date.

MOWING ROADS READY
FOR REAPER

8

CORN HARVEST

The sower went forth sowing
    The seed in secret slept
Through weeks of faith and patience
    Till out the green blade crept;
And warmed by golden sunshine,
    And fed by silver rain,
At last the fields were whiten'd
    To harvest once again.

Hymn - W.St. Hill Bourne

The greatest event of the year was the corn harvest, into which activity the whole neighbourhood became gradually involved.

The first sign of harvest would be the hearing of snippets of information that Farmer X had started a 'road round' and this was followed by another farmer, and then another, until eventually everyone was fully launched into the work.

Watch was kept on fields approaching ripeness and the mowing of the 'road round' would indicate that cutting time was at hand.

In the case of a heavy crop the job of mowing a road round required considerable effort and provided a real indication of the stamina required by men who, working in gangs, had had to mow whole fields before the advent of the reaping machine. A scythe was not everyone's 'cup of tea,' and learning to use one effectively took considerable time and patience.

To be worked comfortably a scythe had to be set to suit the operator's height and reach. A man's height affected the angle of the blade with the ground, and his reach would affect the position of the cogs on the sned.

A certain amount of pleasurable satisfaction could be gained by making a good job of mowing. Armed with a sharp well-hung scythe in a standing crop, a mower progressed with short, sliding steps in time with each rasping sweep of his blade.

THE DAYS OF MANUAL REAPING

The severed corn, falling obliquely, would be carried round by the 'heel,' and its bracing stay, to lie in a neat continuous swath to the mower's left hand.

When gangs of mowers contracted to mow fields, each mower would have a 'picker up' or 'tier up' who followed him tying up the corn into neat sheaves, thus clearing the way for the next mower of the echelon formation.

It was dry work with the hot sun beating down on the men's backs and so, in those seemingly far off days, a generous supply of home-brewed beer was sent to the harvest fields and this practice carried on, on a somewhat diminishing scale, well into the mechanised period of harvesting.

The adaptation of the horse-drawn mowing machine for cutting corn was a monumental advance over hand mowing, and my earliest memories are of this machine, known as a reaper, which was an ordinary mowing machine with reaping attachments which could be fitted as an addition at corn harvest.

These fittings comprised an extra seat for the 'knocker off;' a hinged table of wooden slats extending the full width of the 'bed' and actuated by a foot lever; and a larger outrigger and wheel carrying the external end of the 'bed.'

The 'knocker off' sat on the extra seat with a foot in the stirrup of the foot lever and manoeuvred a peculiarly shaped hand rake to collect the falling corn as it was severed by the knife, and direct it neatly back onto the slightly raised table.

When the machine was in motion, in an average crop, a quantity sufficient for one 'shoff' or sheaf, would collect on the table within about three yards. Its removal was achieved by lowering the table and pressing the hand rake very slightly downwards onto the gathered corn, so that sufficient stubble would protrude through the slats of the table to drag the sheaf

CUTTING CORN: MOWING MACHINE WITH REAPING ATTACHMENTS
Note sheaf lying ready to be tied

off. This would be repeated all the way around the field, leaving a row of untied sheaves in the wake of the machine which had to be tied by hand and thrown clear as each circuit was being made.

To make the cutting operation continuous a number of men would divide the perimiter of the cutting patch into equal lengths so that each had a fair share of tying to do.

Tying up a 'shoff' was done by means of a handful of straws which were passed round it in the form of a 'bond' to be deftly tied by twisting and tucking under.

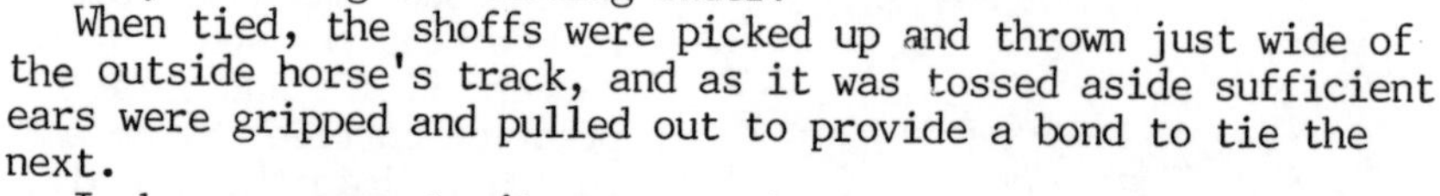

When tied, the shoffs were picked up and thrown just wide of the outside horse's track, and as it was tossed aside sufficient ears were gripped and pulled out to provide a bond to tie the next.

In heavy crops the 'knocker off' had to work very hard when virtually every rakeful would be sufficient for a 'shoff.' It was no mean task to co-ordinate leg and arm movements to suit varying conditions, especially the effect of wind, in order to leave 'shoffs' of uniform size for those doing the tying.

As the years went by, an improved type of machine was introduced, known by the descriptive name of 'self-deliverer' which was the forerunner of the self-binder. The self-deliverer was a weird-looking affair, not unlike a mobile windmill, drawn by two or three horses, but unlike on the reaping machine all driving motion was taken from one wheel, and it was kept on an even keel by one outrigger wheel at the far end of the 'bed.'

Only one man was needed to operate this machine and his chief tasks were to control the horses and select the interval of 'knocking off.'

The spectacular part of this machine was centred in the knocking off rakes, or 'sails' as they were called, which were ingeniously driven by means of a train of bevel gears so that they performed the dual task of pushing the severed corn backwards onto the gathering table, and sliding the accumulation away to one side, clear of the track.

THE FIRST REAPER
KNOWN AS A SELF DELIVERER

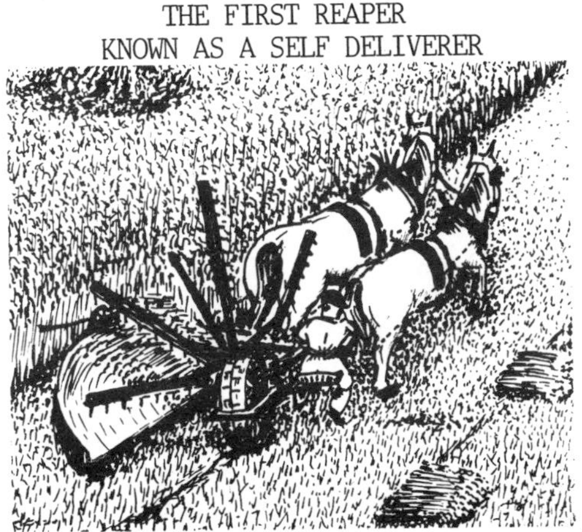

The driver could adjust the sequence of 'knocking off' when the machine was in motion if he wished to do so, and would do so if the density of growth varied. The sail which performed the side delivery sweep was made to drop an extra four or five inches as it passed over the table, thereby taking the untied 'shoff' with it.

This machine made it possible to cut a field without deploying a large gang of tiers; thus at the same time the job of tying could be carried out at a more leisurely pace, and could even be left until the next day, but the whole field of tied shoffs had to be 'stuck up' into 'mows' as soon as possible, since only a well set up 'mow' was reasonably waterproof.

Varieties of corn were 'stuck up' in accepted patterns and could easily be distinguished by the number of shoffs in their arrangement.

Wheat was arranged in eight shoffs per mow - four on each side.

Oats were arranged in six shoffs per mow - two on each side and one at each end.

Barley was arranged in seven shoffs per mow - three each side and one resting lengthwise on the top.

Rye was arranged in six shoffs per mow - two each side and one at each end and the tops tied with a bond - or perhaps a seventh shoff was inverted over the mow and tied with a bond near its butt ends.

The aim in erecting mows was to make them reasonably waterproof and yet open enough below to ensure maximum ventilation. Added to this was the necessity for them to withstand a reasonable amount of wind. There was no task on a farm more unpleasant than re-erecting fallen mows, the shoffs having become tangled and thoroughly saturated.

Corn stayed in the field until most of the sap had dried out of the straw, and during that time it generally received considerable attention from birds - chiefly pigeons, rooks, crows and jackdaws. Good sport could be had with a gun, if one took the trouble to make a 'hide' and had the time to man it.

THE SELF BINDER

When the corn was ready, carting would commence with every available man and vehicle on the job. Work started when the morning dew had evaporated and continued until dusk, with only short pauses for meals and feeding the horses.

Load after load creaked its way towards the stack yard to be unloaded, and no sooner was one stack finished than another started to take shape - always set on plenty of surplus bottom material such as hedge trimmings or straw, to prevent damp rising to spoil the grain.

I well remember the feeling of satisfaction as the last load left the last field; this seemed to be an assurance that, come what may, the main winter food supply was secure. The final act would be the harvesting of the rakings which would generally be stacked by themselves in a convenient place for threshing out first, for fowl corn.

In earlier times when mowing by hand was the only method of cutting corn, a considerable quantitly would be left scattered about and this was left for the gleaners who had it free for the trouble of picking it up.

The season of harvest was considered over when the Harvest Festival had taken place, with its fervent renderings of well known hymns. With churches lavishly decorated with floral tributes and offerings of choice produce, this seemed a fitting end to the year. Only those experienced in the vagaries of wind and weather on farm work can fully appreciate the meaning in the words of such hymns as "We plough the fields and scatter," or "Come ye faithful people, come."

Quite often, after harvest, mobile pens would be taken out onto the stubble fields so that the fowl could pick up the fallen grain, and it was someone's job to visit these free-ranging poultry, night and morning, to lock and unlock them. Even so, it was not uncommon to find a typically brazen fox had thieved a fowl or two in broad daylight.

At this time a start would be made to work the stubbles either by shallow (ebb) ploughing, or breaking up with the cultivator. This work constituted the preliminary working for the following year's root crop and was mainly intended to prevent weeds from becoming too firmly established during autumn.

At these times most of the cleared cornfields would suddenly become adorned with a miscellaneous collection of well spaced bushes. Close inspection would reveal that each one was, in fact, a branch cut from a hedge and set firmly into the ground. This curious array was the work of game-keepers responsible for the prevention of poaching.

Poachers, on cleared cornfields, would be solely after partridges when the young would be almost full grown. Partridge are ground-roosting, and always form up into a close circle facing outwards, so that in an emergency they can take off in the dark without risk of collision. Poachers knew this and it was a relatively simple matter for two of them to walk a field over with a long net dragging (or nearly dragging) the ground in between them, so that a startled covey would become entangled. The rash of thorn bushes prevented - or at least seriously interfered with - such profitable activities.

By mid-October, the job of rick thatching would be well underway and was usually the task of one man. His thatching straw would have been prepared earlier from battens of, preferably, rye straw. Preparation of the straw was known as 'dressing' and involved combing out all short and broken straws to leave only long and straight material for binding up into handy-sized battens.

Before starting, the thatcher would finish off the rick roof by placing a line of straw battens along the crest and securing each overlap with a long thatch peg. Thatching commenced at one end of a roof, after suitable string mooring pegs had been inserted into the gable end at selected intervals.

The maximum width of roof covered at each ladder shift would not exceed thirty inches and covering was started at the eave line, using straw with eave ends pointing upwards for the first layer across, but reversing this direction for all other overlaying courses, up to the crest. (See drawing page 50)

Specially woven thatching string wound on short pegs was un-spooled as covering progressed, being hitched securely around the head end of each peg in its line. As a variation, a thatcher would sometimes cross the thatching string to form diamond patterns between two rows of pegs.

Ricks intended to remain unused until the spring would have more care lavished on their thatch, since it would have to withstand the worst winter gales without being ripped off.

9

ROOT HARVEST AND WINTER TASKS

When as the chilly rocko blows
And winter tells a heavy tale
When Pyes and Daws and Rooks and Crows
Sit cursing of the frost and snows
Then give me ale.

Old Song

October ushered in the season for harvesting root crops and maincrop potatoes, usually acting as a curtain-raiser for this phase of the farming year.

During the preceding weeks, callers would have enquired about the possibility of being employed for 'potato getting,' as it was called, on a piece-work basis. We usually had a couple of Irishmen (father and son) who came to us each year, this being their last job of work before returning home.

Potatoes were generally clamped or 'hogged' on the field, with about thirty to forty rows of potatoes going to one line of clamps. They were usually sorted for size when picked up; the ware size for sale as best quality being put into the clamps and seed sizes interred in smaller clamps, located at one end of each main clamp.

Clamps were made by excavating a smooth slope-sided trench, approximately 30 inches wide by about 12 inches deep, on a previously cleared site, midway between the ridges. This was filled up with potatoes as lifting proceeded, until it was several yards long, but tubers were never exposed to sunlight and air for any lengthy period. Initial covering was with clean straw which was, in turn, covered by soil, leaving odd wisps protruding along the top, to act as ventilators - these were completely closed up as the colder weather came along.

If it was intended to hold on to the crop until February or later, the whole crop would probably be moved to a permanent clamp site, usually near a road and safely re-interred in a much deeper excavation.

By mid-October the mangol harvest was in full swing and upon the success of this job depended the ability to provide sufficient food for cattle during the critical months of February, March and April. This crop was particularly sensitive to frost and every effort was made to harvest it in good order.

The clamp was generally situated near the farm, in a remote part of the rickyard which could be spared for this purpose.

The mangols would be arranged in one or two neat ranks, usually one cart-load 'thick' thrown up well in order to form a sharp crest and covered like potatoes.

Mangols still in the clamp at the end of March would sprout excessively and soil would have to be removed in yard-wide strips to lower the temperature inside.

During late October and November the turnip crop became in need of attention but not with the same urgency, since this crop was largely immune to frost. Swede turnips provided the bulk of early and mid-winter stock food and consequently a good acreage was always sown. Of this acreage almost half would be 'topped' and put into small clamps, each containing one good cart load. These clamps were not trenched in, but were simply constructed on the surface and covered lightly with straw and soil.

If sheep were going to feed from such a crop, it was common practice to take out approximately every alternate twenty ridges for use at the farm, thus leaving a small quantity for the sheep and ensuring that the ground would not be too heavily manured during their staged transit across the field.

Topping turnips and propelling them towards a heap in a truly skilled manner was an art not easily learned, and efforts to master it often resulted in seriously cut fingers.

After surplus root growth had been removed the turnip was first made to swing backwards, letting about six inches of the top slide through the hand as it did so. The reverse swing

HOEING TURNIPS

forward was assisted by a slight pulling effort dependent on the size and distance to the heap, and at the correct moment the top would be cleanly severed, leaving the turnip free to describe a neat arc through the air on its way to the heap.

The knack of topping turnips in this manner centred on the use of the 'topper.' This was held more or less stationary while the turnip's leafy stem was smartly projected against its sharp edge.

Sheep were generally put onto roots when their usual pastures had become short of herbage in late autumn, the principal object being to fatten and get good carcase weight.

Running sheep on roots is recognised as an excellent and well established method of putting valuable manure back into the soil. If they were being corned as well, droppings would be all the richer; therefore care had to be taken not to make the soil too 'fat,' otherwise the following season's corn crop would be too rank and fall flat whilst still green, never to recover.

Iron hurdles were used to fence the field, in such a manner that the sheep could be given a sufficient 'heading' each day. Moving the hurdles was anything but pleasant on either wet or frosty days, and snow made things even worse. Getting to the sheep with supplies of hay and corn through a deep snow was also a formidable task and feeding would take some hours. On the other hand, in clear, hard, frosty conditions, the sheep would frolic around like young lambs at the sight of their breakfast supplies. The thunder of their feet on the iron-hard ground sounded like a minature buffalo stampede.

This daily task was not in any way monotonous. There was always something worth seeing each morning, if only the tracks of some night-prowling animal. Often one would have the pleasure of seeing the most wonderful sunrise, with effects varying from gossamer-like tracery, picked out with spun gold, to the more massive winter's cloudheads, so soon to bring rain.

In hard weather, quite a good cross-section of the native bird population could be seen gathering around the empty sheep troughs to pick up scraps of meal and corn.

Frosty weather in January, February or March was usually the time when the bulk of 'muck' carting took place. Each day, heavily laden carts would journey from the farmyard to the field, where the waggoner would unload them to form long rows of uniform heaps.

When quite small I was presented with a large and beautiful model of a horse and cart and this I treasured. One day, seeing the men engaged upon manure carting I elected to join them, with the result that I soon became bogged down with my odourous load. Alas! my gaily decorated outfit and myself needed a thorough wash before we were even remotely acceptable in the family circle again.

During late autumn, winter and in very early spring, a general effort would be made to eliminate or reduce the rabbit population, by ferreting, trapping and snaring.

Ferreting was the most popular method where a farmer's own resident rabbits were concerned, an activity which provided plenty of rough sport for both gun and dog when rabbits 'bolted' well. On the other hand considerable digging became necessary if rabbits remained underground in the 'bury.' To ensure that the ferrets were really active they would have been 'clemmed' since early the previous day, and to prevent them fastening onto a rabbit they would be neatly 'coped' - with string.

Rabbits cornered in blind holes had to be dug for, and to find these use was made of a line-ferret which, it was hoped, would eventually hole up with any cornered rabbit. Working a 'liner' always involved a lot of listening and ground crawling in an attempt to locate any subterranean bumps and scratchings; sometimes line-ferrets had a bell attached to their collars.

Trapping was quite extensively used to keep one's own rabbit population in check and proved very effective if carried out regularly, but it must be admitted that the 'gin' trap was a cruel device and it is now illegal. (See drawing on page 15)

The use of snares was of a more universal value since resident or visiting rabbits could be dealt with equally well. A good deal of strategy was necessary to determine the habits of a particular rabbit colony before one attempted to lay snares. It had to be established where their food supply lay and their route to and from it had to be known. Then the ideal set for snares was out in the open and about midway between food and warren area. Rabbits travel fast and purposefully along well defined runs during the hours of darkness.

Professional poachers worked by night. For rabbits and hares they used long line nets which were skilfully and silently set between the place where the animals were feeding and their warren or cover. With the nets down, success depended upon a well trained dog, which was sent to ghost around the outskirts of the area to scare rabbits homewards. Their headlong rush carried them into obstructing nets.

Successful poaching depended upon an intimate knowledge of the animals' habits together with a good nose for wind and weather, and NOT least an idea of the whereabouts of the farmer or keeper on any particular night.

Winter work on a farm was very much contolled by the varying weather conditions. Generally speaking, the bulk of the backend ploughing and stubble working would have been finished by the time the last of the root crops were under cover.

Christmas would see the work largely reduced to tending livestock and doing odd jobs like threshing and carting roots for cattle food and visits to the local mill. Bad days were used for cleaning out granaries and lofts, or doing maintenance jobs on implements.

Hedge laying was carried out during the early part of the year, and more often than not done by a professional hedger on a piece-work basis. It was a real art and it took a long time to acquire the master touch - a touch which was marked by an ability to tackle any kind of hedge and make a good job of it. The principal object in laying a hedge was to bring about a uniform thickening of the material in the bottom and to restore the shape and size, making it suitable for annual trimming.

A very definite first requirement in a newly layed hedge was that it should all live and produce new growth in the spring.

A young hedge layed much more easily than an old one and nothing looked better than a new hawthorn hedge after its first laying, especially when willow or hazel 'heatherings' had been uniformly laced through the top of the stakes to keep the layed material from rising up.

Hedges which had been layed several times times before were all the more difficult to handle for this reason, but an experienced man could make a marvellous job of a seemingly impossible hedge by cunningly making up the gaps and making the most of what growing material was available. The finishing touch to the work would be provided by rebuilding the hedge bank and turning over the top sod to

HEDGE LAYING - EARLY SPRING

retard the growth of grass and weed until new hedge shoots were firmly established. This banking up could be compared with the effect of mounting a good picture in a fitting frame.

It was important not to set any 'pleacher' down below the true horizontal since sap does not travel downhill. For this reason the direction of laying would have to be changed to suit this requirement where hedges traversed changing contours.

If required, suitable straight growers would be left, at forty to fifty yard intervals to grow and provide strong, sturdy rick props for cutting down in a year or two's time.

The task of hedge laying was rewarding in many ways because it was fundamentally creative and would stand as a living example of a man's work for years to come. On the job, it was customary to work singlehanded taking lunch, picnic fashion, after lighting a fire on the leeward side of the hedge.

I have pleasant memories of sitting by a crackling fire, singeing bacon in the flame or toasting cheese on the clean blade of a spade, while the searching March wind tried in vain to disturb my small creature comforts.

Spring would see young shoots breaking on the newly laid hedge - but the time to judge the work would be at the end of August when only the shoots on the best and correctly pleached growers would have succeeded in establishing themselves to provide the foundation of the new hedge.

All over the farm this quickening of spring would herald the beginning of yet another year, marking the time when the fruits of earlier work and planning should begin to show forth.

Good farmers tended to keep their skilled labour force intact for years, while a few were constantly advertising for men, signifying that all was not well between master and man. Farmers and smallholders moved perhaps even less frequently, and news of a pending move was first read in local papers in the form of an auctioneer's sale notice, setting out the main items of live and dead farming stock for disposal.

The day of the sale would see great activity with all the stock-in-trade being arranged in orderly rows in an adjacent field while a cattle sale ring would be set up somewhere within the farm premises - big sales would sometimes include a refreshment tent.

If the sale were on a big farm it could run into two days, but this was unusual, and normally selling was over in one. People would come from far and near, some to buy, some to look on and others there for the chance bargain.

I used to enjoy visiting a sale and listening to the patter of the auctioneers, one of whom was quite a character, and dressed in grey tweed breeches, black leggings and boots, and wore a bowler hat.

When really warmed up he could wheedle bids from the most unlikely people. Having a good turn of earthy wit, he drew folk around him, particularly when selling household goods, where among his pet items were those articles of chinaware which usually reside underneath beds. Here he would find cause to remark upon their size and state of ornateness and usually finished off by informing those present that they never knew when the need might arise and therefore they should not be shy in bidding. His choice of expressions added that little extra spice in a somewhat puritanical society.

Farmers on estate farms who moved or retired had to comply with certain tenancy agreements. The outgoing farmer could sell or take virtually everything belonging to him with the exception of manure and straw from the previous year's harvest. This stayed behind for the new tenant, so that there would be no serious impoverishmnet of the land as a result of the change.

The tenancy agreement also required that hedges and fences be put into serviceable condition, while ditches and water-courses had to be capable of draining flood water away without any back pounding or damming up.

If an outgoing farmer had recently applied artificial manure, or limed or 'marled' (applied clay to) fields, he could claim for un-exhausted improvements. This action, however, usually led to the appointment of arbitrators, when it was quite usual for the estate agent to lodge counterclaims, based on the state of the farm - including weed infestation and the condition of drains, ditches and fences.

Memories of the time before mechanisation seem to show that farming and farmwork followed a well tried pattern and, where the land permitted, heavy crops were produced.

Large and small farms alike worked a six day week in the fields but the working day was longer, especially when the hours of daylight permitted. In general there were more acres under the plough and milking herds were not so numerous, but on the other hand more beef cattle were produced.

Farms employed more men - and women, who worked on the land as well as indoors. Married men generally lived in tied cottages, while single men 'lived in,' in the large farmhouses which are now so inconvenient.

Perhaps one of the most unattractive features of modern agricultural mechanisation is the fact that ordinary farm work has become a very lonely occupation. Gone are the days when farmers employed between perhaps three and twelve or more full-time workmen. Numbers such as these ensured that men worked in company on main tasks; consequently work was less monotonous because conversation and co-operation were possible.

By comparison, the modern farmworker leads a muted existence. He is more often than not alone in a field, and even if not conversation is impossible owing to the noise of tractors. The same noise blots out all other sounds, particularly the bird song.

Farmworkers of the past were, generally speaking, light hearted and extrovert, and it is regrettable that accelerated mechanisation of farm work has, indirectly, produced a group of people who resemble Robinson Crusoe in their measure of loneliness during their working day.

Though work was hard it was not one long rush, yet it was inevitable that mechanisation should come, bringing vast changes to the farming scene.

Because of this I count it a privilege to have had the good fortune to witness the change and to retain memories of a departed yet nostalgic age.

A SECRET JOY

We who were born
In country places
Far from cities
And shifting faces,
We have a birthright
No man can sell
And a secret joy
No man can tell

For we are kindred
To lonely things.

Thought to be the work of
Charles Morgan

ILLUSTRATIONS

	Page
HARVEST	Front cover
STONE HOUSE FARM	4
MAP	4
A TWO-BUCKET WELL	8
WOOD-FIRED BAKE OVEN	12
RENDERING DOWN LARD	13
TOOLS	15
STEAM THRESHING MACHINE	18
CHURNS	23
NO GAPS IN THIS HEDGE	28
TYPICAL WELL BUILT LOAD OF CORN	34
BREW HOUSE AND BAKE HOSUE	38
THE SINGLE FURROW PLOUGH	41
IN MY FATHER'S FOOTSTEPS	44
THE ART OF SOWING BROADCAST	46
THE ART OF THATCHING	50
MOWING ROADS READY FOR REAPER	51
THE DAYS OF MANUAL REAPING	53
CUTTING CORN: MOWING MACHINE WITH REAPING ATTACHMENTS	54
THE FIRST REAPER: KNOWN AS SELF DELIVERER	55
THE SELF BINDER	56
HOEING TURNIPS	59
HEDGE LAYING: EARLY SPRING	62

Drawings from memory, by the Author

GLOSSARY

Including many Shropshire words

Boosey	-	Brick or cement feeding trough for stall-fed cattle
Buck	-	Adjustable towing point on horse-drawn plough or similar implement
Butt or Bunt	-	Bump heads together, practised by certain animals
Butter mit	-	Shallow vessel on which butter kneaded
Cade	-	Hand-reared lamb
Casting	-	See Reon
Causey	-	Causeway or small paved yard
Chain harrow	-	Harrow for general purposes, ie levelling, collecting, distribution
Clab	-	Thump of horse's foot on stable floor
Clemmed	-	Starved of food
Cogs	-	Two handles of scythe
Commin men	-	Residents on common land
Cop	-	Initial two furrows turned inwards against each other when ploughing starts
Coped	-	Muzzled
Crafts	-	Crofts or small holdings
Dog	-	Falling ratchet
Duff	-	Dough
Ebb ploughing	-	Shallow ploughing
Fingers	-	Fingers' width, when drink is measured
Gathering	-	Ploughing round the cop - see Reon
Gearing	-	Wooden extensions fitted to carts and waggons for harvesting
Grains	-	Spent malt; or the prongs of a pitchfork
Heathering	-	Hazels or willows laced along top of newly-laid hedge
Heavy on	-	Loading of a cart too heavily at front
Heel rake	-	Large rake, pulled by hand to pick up fallen hay or corn - forerunner of horse rake
Hogged	-	Clamped, as potatoes
Hooking to	-	Starting work with a horse team
Knocker-off	-	The man who dropped the sheaves from mower
Light on	-	Loading of cart too heavily at rear
Liner	-	Line ferret, ferret on a line
Mixen	-	Hole for storage of dung
Overshot	-	Mill wheel, where water flows over top to turn it
Peeling	-	Shallow ploughing, maximum depth 2 inches
Pickel	-	Pitch fork

Pleacher	-	Part of hedge left for laying, after clearing
Plough tails	-	Handles of horse-drawn plough
Pruffle	-	Noise made by horse when clearing its nose
Reon or Rheon	-	Final splitting of narrow unploughed strip of land to leave uniformly straight depression. When unploughed ground between two gatherings becomes the narrower strip, the ploughman circuits this portion until he comes to his Reon - this is known as Casting
Ripples	-	Wooden side members fitted to carts or lorries for small animals to be carried safely
Road round	-	First round of corn field to be mown
Scratchings	-	Solid residue left after rendering down lard
Scuffle	-	Implement for removing weeds between row crops eg turnips
Seed hopper	-	Container used for broadcast sowing
Shandray	-	High horse-drawn trap
Shell board	-	Curved casting on plough, which turns the furrow over
Ship	-	Local name for sheep
Skelp	-	Implement added to plough for digging in manure
Shoff	-	Corn sheaf
Skippit	-	Ditching tool
Sned	-	Shaft on a scythe
Stank or Stake	-	Light wooden post for fencing purposes
Suff	-	Culvert or large drain
Swake	-	Swivelling bracket to support cooking pots over an open fire
Tailing stick	-	Iron crook for lifting and clearing drag harrow
Tub	-	Low-slung, rounded, horse-drawn conveyance, which could be elaborately made
Tun dish	-	Funnel
Ullert	-	Any owl
Undershot	-	Mill wheel, where water flows under it to turn it
Whipple/Swingle tree	-	Used to connect draw chains (behind horse) to implement
Witch	-	Large wooden bin for grain
Writing master	-	Yellow hammer - eggs marked with curious black scrawl
Yilve	-	Four or five pronged fork - mainly for potato lifting
Yockle	-	Green woodpecker